W9-CEL-642

AN AMERICAN H·E·R·O

ALSO BY BARRY DENENBERG:

Voices from Vietnam

The True Story of J. Edgar Hoover
and the FBI

Nelson Mandela:
"No Easy Walk to Freedom"

Stealing Home:
The Story of Jackie Robinson

John Fitzgerald Kennedy:
America's 35th President

AN
AMERICAN
H·E·R·O

THE

True

Story of

Charles A.

Lindbergh

BARRY DENENBERG

SCHOLASTIC
HARDCOVER

SCHOLASTIC INC.   NEW YORK

Copyright acknowledgments can be found on pages 253–54 and 255.

Copyright © 1996 by Barry Denenberg.
All rights reserved. Published by Scholastic Inc.,
555 Broadway, New York, NY 10012.
SCHOLASTIC HARDCOVER and the SCHOLASTIC HARDCOVER
logo are registered trademarks of Scholastic Inc.

No part of this publication may be reproduced,
or stored in a retrieval system, or transmitted in any form
or by any means, electronic, mechanical, photocopying, recording,
or otherwise, without written permission of the publisher.
For information regarding permission,
write to Scholastic Inc.,
555 Broadway, New York, NY 10012.

Library of Congress Cataloging-in-Publication Data
Denenberg, Barry.
An American hero : the true story of Charles A. Lindbergh / Barry
Denenberg.
p.   cm.
Includes bibliographical references and index.
ISBN 0-590-46923-1 (alk. paper)
1. Lindbergh, Charles A. (Charles Augustus), 1902–1974.   2. Air
pilots—United States—Biography.   I. Title.
TL540.L5D476   1996
629.13'092—dc20

[B]   95-24628
                                                                  CIP
                                                                   AC

12 11 10 9 8 7 6 5 4 3 2 1   6 7 8 9/9 0 1/0

                    Printed in the U.S.A.   37

First printing, April 1996
Design by Elizabeth B. Parisi
Photo research by Deborah Thompson Kurosz
Production supervision by Angela Biola

For Gregg Quinn

CONTENTS

THE PRIZE

Time: 7:52 A.M.
Date: FRIDAY, MAY 20, 1927
Place: ROOSEVELT FIELD, LONG ISLAND

Twenty-five-year-old airmail pilot Charles Lindbergh is about to take off on a rain-soaked runway. He is attempting to become the first person to fly across the Atlantic Ocean from New York to Paris alone.

In 1919, Raymond Orteig, a Frenchman, offered a $25,000 prize to the first aviator to fly nonstop, from New York to Paris or Paris to New York. After eight years no one had won the Orteig prize.

In the intervening years, however, engines had been made more powerful and more reliable, and the design of the planes had improved. It was now feasible to cross the Atlantic by air. By 1926 there were a number of serious contenders for the prize.

That year, Lieutenant Commander Richard Byrd became the first man to fly over the North Pole. With $100,000 in backing, the now famous Byrd began preparing his transatlantic flight.

Frenchman René Fonck was a glamorous World War I ace. (In fact, as a child Charles Lindbergh had followed Fonck's exploits.) His tri-motor plane was big and luxuriously appointed. Fonck had gone so far as to hire an interior decorator. The seats were upholstered in red leather, and there was a sofa bed on board, as well as a refrigerator, hot meals, croissants, and champagne for the anticipated victory celebration in Paris.

Test pilot Clarence Chamberlin and stunt pilot Bert Acosta would be flying the Columbia, *which some considered the best plane. They had recently set a new world-endurance record, flying 51 hours, 11 minutes, and 25 seconds.*

Lieutenant Commander Noel Davis and Charles Nungesser, another French ace, were also preparing to fly the Atlantic.

After years of inactivity it now seemed likely that someone would win the prize. Whoever took off first would most likely have the edge.

However, all had not gone according to plan. In fact, one tragic accident after another shook up the field and cleared the way for the dark horse, Lindbergh.

First Fonck.

His plane was unable to attain the 80-mph airspeed necessary for takeoff. As the plane bounced over the ruts that crossed the runway, parts began to fly off and the tail dragged on the ground, sending dust into the air. Finally Fonck's plane tumbled into a gully at the end of the runway and burst into flames as a stunned crowd watched. Fonck and his navigator got out before the gasoline exploded. But his mechanic and radio operator did not. They both burned to death.

Next Byrd.

His huge (71-foot wingspan) three-engine plane, the America, crashed on landing during a test flight. Everyone except the pilot was injured. And the crash was only the beginning of Byrd's problems. One of his biggest financial backers was now insisting on further testing. Byrd's takeoff was delayed until the tests had been completed.

Chamberlin, too, was unable to take off. He had mechanical, financial, and legal problems. The legal controversy led to a court order that kept the Columbia *locked in an airplane hangar.*

Davis was able to take off, but not much else. Overweight by nearly 2,000 pounds, his plane lumbered down the runway barely avoiding some trees (trees it had cleared easily during a previous test flight), lost altitude, dove, and crashed into a swamp. Davis and his copilot, Lieutenant Stanton Wooster, trapped in the cockpit, died.

On the other side of the ocean, Nungesser had taken off from Paris, headed for New York. His single-engine plane, the White Bird, *was driven by a 450-horsepower engine. Unlike Fonck, Byrd, and Davis, Nungesser had stripped down his plane — even going as far as jettisoning the landing gear after takeoff to reduce wind resistance. He planned to land in New York Harbor.*

The White Bird *had been sighted over Ireland, Newfoundland, Nova Scotia, and as close as Portland, Maine. Back in France Nungesser's fellow citizens had already begun celebrating.*

But these early sightings, except in Newfoundland, would turn out to be untrue. Nungesser and François Coli, his copilot, would never be heard from again. Rescue planes were still searching for them as Lindbergh prepared to take off.

Only a short time before it had seemed certain that Lindbergh would not get his chance — that Fonck, Byrd, Chamberlin, or Davis would succeed before him.

Now, as Lindbergh readies his tiny, speedy silver plane, the Spirit of St. Louis, *he knows that six men have died doing what he is about to attempt.*

If he fails, chances are he, too, will die. If he succeeds, he will win the Orteig prize and worldwide recognition. If he succeeds, his life will change forever and he will never be able to look back.

PART ONE: ASCENT

He is and always will be not merely a schoolboy hero, but a schoolboy.

— Harold Nicholson, writer

Chapter One

$\mathcal{G}$ ROWING $\mathcal{U}$ P

Life's values originate in circumstances over which the individual has no control.

— Charles Lindbergh

C.A. AND EVANGELINE

Charles August Lindbergh was born in Sweden and came to America when he was an infant. His father changed the family name from Månsson because he felt too many Swedes were named Månsson; the name was so common that it had become a nuisance. He chose Lindberg, which was a name other Månssons had already adopted, and added an h. For most of his life Charles August was known as C.A.

C.A.'s first wife died after eight years of marriage. They had two surviving children, Lillian and Eva. By that time C.A. was one of the wealthiest men in Little Falls, Min-

Charles Lindbergh's parents, Evangeline Lodge Land, age 22, and Charles August Lindbergh, age 41.

nesota (pop. 5,000). He developed a reputation as a good lawyer and a man of integrity. Soon many of Little Falls's most successful businesses were his clients.

Within a year of his first wife's death, in 1901, he remarried. His new wife, Evangeline Lodge Land, was from Detroit, Michigan. She was a college graduate hired to teach science courses in the Little Falls High School. She was pretty, confident, and sophisticated — an easterner come to the rugged West. At twenty-four, she was seventeen years younger than C.A.

Charles Augustus Lindbergh was born in Detroit on February 4, 1902, and grew up on a 110-acre farm on the banks of the Mississippi River, just outside of Little Falls. His father hired men to work there, as well as a cook, a nurse, and a maid to help his mother. Although his half sisters also lived on the farm, as far as Charles was concerned they were girls and were too old to be playmates anyway. (Lillian was fourteen years older, and Eva ten.) Much of his childhood he spent alone, except for the companionship of the family dogs. One of the most dramatic events of Charles Lindbergh's early childhood occurred when he was three and a half.

While he was playing in the house, a fire broke out. The nurse picked him up and ran from the house, telling Charles not to look. But he did, and saw the house as it burned to the ground. The next day he returned.

I hold Mother's hand tightly while she speaks, looking down on the still smoldering ruins. It's the next day. Our entire house has sunk into the stone walls of its basement. I recognize our cookstove, under pipes behind the furnace. Next to it are twisted bedsteads. There's the hot-water boiler. There's the laundry sink. Everything is covered with the gray snow of ashes. Right at my feet is a melted, green-glass lump that was once a windowpane. Out of the pit, smoke-smutted but sharp-cut against thick leaves and sky, rises our brick chimney, tall and spindly without a house around it. And on the chimney mantelpiece, midway up its height, where the big living room once ended, is Mother's Mexican idol — a small, red-clay figure — the only object to pass undamaged through the fire. Of course some clothes and books were saved, and the

Charles Lindbergh,
age 14 months.

men carried out a few pieces of furniture. But my toys, and the big stairs, and my room above the river, are gone forever . . .

— Charles Lindbergh

After the fire Charles and his family lived in a hotel and, later, an apartment in Minneapolis while a new house was being built. Charles missed the farm and the house and was eager to return to Little Falls. Even when the new house was completed, however, it was a disappointment. Although it had ten rooms, it was only half the size of the old one and just didn't feel the same.

By this time Charles had to endure another traumatic event. C.A. and Evangeline had recognized that their marriage had fallen apart. C.A. insisted, however, that they could not get a divorce or legal separation or make any public acknowledgment of their situation. He did this for a number of reasons. For one, he wanted to maintain a relationship with his only son. But he also believed divorce would be viewed, at the time, as a radical step — radical enough to ruin his new career in national government.

In 1906, C.A. was elected to the United States Congress as a representative from Minnesota's Sixth District. To protect his career he and Evangeline agreed to live separately while keeping up appearances as best they could.

The Lindberghs, including Lillian and Eva, lived in Washington, D.C., beginning in 1907. During the day, C.A. went to the House of Representatives, and Charles to school. After school Charles usually visited his father, spending hours on the floor of the House of Representatives, which he found stifling — like church, to which he

Lindbergh with his father, C. A., on the floor of Congress.

had refused to go. He also spent time "helping out" with office tasks and generally irritating the staff.

In the summers he and his mother took the train back to the farm in Little Falls. On the way they always visited his mother's home in Detroit, often staying for weeks at a time.

GRANDFATHER LAND

Charles's grandfather was a dentist and inventive genius who pioneered the use of porcelain in dental crowns and wrote two books on dentistry. He also invented a self-bouncing cradle (which Charles used when he was a baby), an air-filtration system (because Grandfather believed that the recently invented automobile was polluting Detroit's air), and other household contrivances.

Dr. Charles H. Land, without even attending high school, had become quite well known as a dentist. His lack of formal education, coupled with his feisty and eccentric personality, caused the dental profession to denounce him. The State of Illinois refused to issue him a license. He accused the dental establishment of being more interested in making money than in practicing proper dentistry. He brought a number of libel suits against his opponents, one of which forced Grandfather Land himself into bankruptcy.

Grandfather Land's house doubled as his laboratory and office. The basement and other rooms contained all kinds of fascinating equipment. Charles spent countless hours watching his grandfather in his workshop and admiring the many things he could do with his hands. Grandfather Land patiently answered Charles's questions and allowed him to roam about, satisfying his curiosity. Only dangerous instruments and chemicals were off-limits.

At dinner Charles listened as his maverick grandfather talked about religion, politics, the origins of life, and the latest mechanical scientific inventions. Charles considered his grandfather a wise man and enjoyed the time he and his mother spent in Detroit.

ON THE MOVE

During summers back in Little Falls, Charles's father would visit, though he lived separately from Charles and his

mother. He and Charles would go fishing and hunting together — Charles already owned a .22 caliber rifle (his
grandfather had given it to him when Charles was six), a
12-gauge shotgun, and a .38 caliber revolver. By the time he
was thirteen he could outshoot his father. C.A. also taught
his son to swim:

I was eight years old then. We were near our big, red
granite "drying-rock," and stripped naked. We almost
never wore bathing suits on the river bank, for there
was rarely anybody within sight. One day, I waded out
neck-deep on the slimy, smooth-stone bottom, and
slipped into a hole that was over my head. When I
broke the surface and coughed in a breath of air, I was
startled to find that my father wasn't running toward
me. He just stood on shore and laughed. And then I

Lindbergh poses after a
successful hunt with his father.

realized that I was swimming by myself. The current quickly carried me to shallow water.

— Charles Lindbergh

Charles enjoyed the time he spent with his father. However, he spent most of his time with his mother, and they grew close. Rarely was he with both of them at once. Of all the photographs of Charles Lindbergh there is not one of him with his mother and father. Charles moved around so much (Little Falls, Detroit, Washington) that he had to attend eleven different schools — never completing a full year in any one of them. He and his mother would often arrive in Washington after the school year had begun. And, just as often, they would leave before it ended. School didn't interest him very much, anyway. He was not inspired by what was being taught and he studied very little. His mind often wandered from the classroom to the things that truly interested him: the farm in Little Falls, the outdoors, and all things mechanical.

Charles showed exceptional mechanical ability by the time he was nine. He took things apart — his bicycle, for instance — and reassembled them with ease. He once conceived and built a clever and elaborate mechanical system for transporting large blocks of ice that had been cut from the Mississippi and were stored in the icehouse.

With week-apart food deliveries from town, an icebox was quite important to us. In addition to meat and vegetables, the icebox let us keep fresh milk. . . . It was my job to fill the box with ice, and in the early years this was a formidable task because of the weight of the ice. (I felt it beneath my dignity to split the cakes in half.)

— Charles Lindbergh

Using wooden planks for a slide, wire, rope, a cart, tongs, and a pulley system, he accomplished his task.

He enjoyed doing things with his hands and learning how engines worked. And, of course, there were those many visits with Grandfather Land. Charles wanted to get out of the theoretical world of the classroom and into the practical world.

When Charles was eleven his father bought a Model T Ford for campaign trips and family use. Discovering that his legs didn't quite reach the pedals, Charles did exercises he thought might remedy the situation. Once they did reach, he began driving, looking through the steering wheel to see the road ahead. He sped over rutted, rural Minnesota roads (licenses were not yet required) and explored the country-side surrounding Little Falls. He and his mother went on day trips, packing a picnic lunch.

When his father came to prepare for an upcoming election, Charles picked him up at the station in the new car. His father let him drive it on weekends as long as he acted responsibly. Charles learned to repair flat tires, adjust carbu-retors, and do whatever had to be done to keep the engine running.

Politically, C.A. had come to represent those Americans who believed that the banks, big business, and other finan-cial institutions were pushing the United States into World War I solely to make money. He even published two books at his own expense. They explained his views on reforming the country's financial structure and why he was against America's involvement in World War I.

Charles was thrilled to be allowed to drive his father, who was trying to sway voters, around the state. But he paid little attention to the speeches, the crowds, and the cheering. Instead he tinkered with the engine and kept careful notes about repairs.

A few years later C.A. lost an election for a Senate seat. Although he still held his seat in the House until the end of the congressional session, his public career seemed to be over. Evangeline no longer saw any reason to keep up appearances.

Evangeline loved to travel, and she decided that she and Charles would spend the winter in California. Although he would miss his father, this plan was fine with Charles. He disliked Washington — the grim, gray winters, the crowded, noisy urban environment, and living in one small rented apartment after another. And, besides, he couldn't bring Dingo, whom he had adopted as an abandoned puppy, to Washington. Each winter Dingo had to be left behind in the care of neighbors.

His mother wanted to go by train, but fourteen-year-old Charles convinced her to let him drive.

Accompanied by his uncle from Detroit, and Wahgoosh, a terrier mix who had replaced Dingo, they set out for California in the summer of 1916. The trip took much longer than they thought it would. At times it rained so hard the wheels could no longer turn because the mud was so deep. Then they would have to stay in hotels, waiting until the roads dried. Charles drove all the way — 1,500 miles. The trip took more than a month.

Lindbergh with his favorite dog, Dingo.

When they finally arrived, Charles was enrolled in yet another school. He continued to be disinterested and distracted — spending time investigating the California seacoast rather than attending class. He didn't participate in sports or extracurricular activities and stayed pretty much to himself. He never spoke up in class and had no friends.

Back home in Little Falls, sixteen-year-old Charles's grades were so bad, it looked as if he might not even graduate from high school. But the government had announced a new program that might help. Because of the lack of able-bodied men (many of whom were off fighting in World War I), any senior who agreed to work full time on his family's farm producing food could automatically graduate high school. Charles convinced his mother to let him work on the farm. He returned to school just long enough to get his diploma and leave.

COLLEGE

For two years Charles devoted himself to running the family farm. He liked working outdoors and did most of the work himself. He took care of the sheep, plowed the fields, mended the fences, repaired the barn, built a shed for the pigs, and helped the pregnant animals give birth. He bought the latest farm machinery, including a state-of-the-art tractor, and built an incubator himself. He even took on a part-time job representing a milking machine company. But the work was grueling, potentially dangerous, and, especially in the years right after World War I, not very profitable.

Charles was, to some degree, unsure what he wanted to do. His mother, however, wasn't. She wanted Charles to go

Lindbergh at the University of Wisconsin.

to college. In large part to please her, he enrolled at the University of Wisconsin to study engineering in 1920.

Charles chose Wisconsin for a number of reasons. For one, it had a good engineering department. It was also relatively close to Little Falls, and there were lakes, which appealed to Charles. His mother was able to get a job there teaching science in the local high school. C.A. paid for the first year's tuition but Evangeline's salary had to pay for everything else.

After finding a tenant for the farm, Charles and his mother moved to a low-rent apartment three blocks from campus.

Charles found that college, like grade school and high school, had little to offer him. The courses didn't interest him and, as always, he didn't study. He was soon placed on academic probation. He considered his fellow students immature, and their interests — drinking, smoking, dancing, and dating — a waste of time. He never had a date during the almost two years he spent in Madison. His classmates considered him odd and surly.

He did participate in one aspect of university life, however. He joined the Reserve Officers' Training Corps (ROTC) and became a member of the pistol and rifle team. He was the best shot and led his team to first place in national competition.

The only two friends he had in college both rode motorcycles, like him. Charles had bought a motorcycle in his last year in high school. He brought it with him to Wisconsin and rode recklessly through the surrounding countryside.

Lindbergh, age 19, on a motorcycle trip to Chicago, 1921.

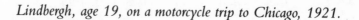

Charles was an accomplished and fearless rider. He even talked about riding his bike off one of the ski jumps.

One day the three friends were passing a street that plunged steeply down to a cross street with a tall fence across it. One of them remarked that a motorcyclist would no doubt crash into the fence if his brakes failed while coming down the hill. Charles, considering this a personal challenge, declared that he could ride his bike safely down the hill and make the sharp turn without having to use his brakes. When the other two said they didn't believe him, Charles decided to show them.

Charles didn't use his brakes, but he couldn't make the turn and took a spill, crashing into the fence. He was cut and bleeding, yet not hurt seriously. He looked up the hill and announced that he knew what he had done wrong. If he had accelerated just as he made the turn he wouldn't have cracked up. Determined and confident, he picked up his undamaged cycle, mounted it, rode back up the hill, and successfully rode down, making the turn without using his brakes.

FLYING

As a child, Charles had daydreamed about flying, and when he was ten years old, had gone with his mother to an air show outside of Washington, D.C. He saw one airplane race an automobile and another drop oranges on the outline of a battleship below. Later he followed the careers of the glamorous World War I aerial aces (aces were pilots who had shot down five or more planes in combat). He was fascinated and decided that someday he wanted to fly.

One of his fellow cyclists had brochures from various flying schools around the country. At the time, flying was considered a disreputable thing to do — certainly an extreme
choice for a vocation. In fact, flying was so dangerous, insurance companies would not issue life insurance policies to
"gypsy pilots," who toured the country putting on exhibi-
tions and taking passengers up for five- and ten-dollar rides.
But a restless Charles Lindbergh had already made up his
mind. His mother tried to persuade him not to do it and
even asked C.A. to help. Both disapproved, and Evangeline
feared she was about to become separated from the son to
whom she had become so attached. But neither parent
would stand in his way.

Charles had already written to an aircraft company
in Lincoln, Nebraska, that offered free lessons to anyone
who bought one of its planes. Charles didn't want to buy a
plane, but they were willing to give him flying lessons for
$500.

By the middle of his sophomore year it looked as if
Charles would be expelled. He didn't wait around to find
out. In late March 1922, he mounted his cycle and headed
for Lincoln, Nebraska.

Chapter Two

WINGS

When I was a child on our Minnesota farm, I spent hours lying on my back . . . hidden from passersby, watching white cumulus clouds drift overhead, staring into the sky. It was a different world up there. You had to be flat on your back, screened in by the grass stalks, to live in it. Those clouds, how far away were they? Nearer than the neighbor's house, untouchable as the moon — unless you had an airplane. How wonderful it would be, I'd thought, if I had an airplane — wings with which I could fly up to the clouds and explore their caves and canyons — wings like that hawk circling above me. Then, I would ride on the wind and be part of the sky . . .

— Charles Lindbergh

ORVILLE AND WILBUR

> I cannot but believe that we stand at the beginning of
> a new era, the Age of Flight.
>
> — Orville Wright

One year after Charles Lindbergh was born, two brothers
from Dayton, Ohio, made the first successful powered flight.

For hundreds of years humans had thought about flying.
In the early 1800s, studies of birds in flight led to the first
gliders. Other pioneers in aviation worked with small models, later translating what they learned to larger, full-sized
planes. Some of them died trying to turn what was considered fantasy into reality.

The Wright brothers had first become interested in flying when Wilbur was eleven and Orville was seven. They
were fascinated by a toy helicopter given to them by their
father. Later, their interest in mechanics led them to own a
bicycle company. At first they just rented and repaired bicycles. But soon, thanks to the bicycle craze of the 1890s, they
expanded and opened new and larger stores where they
built their own custom models.

Orville and Wilbur did not have any formal mechanical
or scientific training. They didn't even have high school
diplomas. But they did have a feel for materials and how
they function, the patience to solve problems, and the capacity to work as a team. These qualities, combined with a
vision and a belief in themselves, led to their momentous
flight on December 17, 1903. At 10:35 A.M., on the sand
dunes of Kitty Hawk, a remote fishing village in North
Carolina (chosen because of the steady wind velocity), their

The Wright brothers' historic first flight. Orville lies prone on the lower wing as Wilbur runs alongside the flyer.

perseverance was rewarded. With a ground speed of about seven miles per hour and an altitude of ten feet, their airplane flew a distance of 120 feet. It was man's first flight.

For twenty years, however, flying remained something only fools and crazy people did.

FLYING SCHOOL

Charles arrived in Lincoln, Nebraska, on April Fools' Day — appropriately, as it turned out.

The first week at Ray Page's Flying School he learned all he could from the mechanics, helping out when asked. He learned how to service a 150-horsepower engine, why planes were designed the way they were, and how to keep them in proper running order.

His first flight was on April 9, 1922. He sat in the open front cockpit, leather helmet over his head and goggles protecting his eyes.

Lindbergh with two other flyers at Ray Page's flying school in Lincoln, Nebraska. The dog on the wing accompanied them on trips around the country.

It was every bit as thrilling as he had hoped.

The roar grows louder. Wings begin to tremble. The engine's power shakes up my legs from the floor boards, beats down on my head from the slipstream, starts a flying wire vibrating. I twist about to look back at the pilot. His eyes study the instruments — no trace of a smile on his face. This is serious business, flying.

The engine quiets. The pilot nods. A mechanic from each side ducks in and unchocks a wheel. We taxi downwind, bumping over sod clumps, to the end of the field. A burst of engine — the tail swings around into the wind. There are seconds of calm while the pilot glances a last time at temperature of water, pressures of oil and air; checks again the direction of wind and clearness of field; makes a slight adjustment to his goggles.

Now! — The roar becomes deafening — the plane lurches forward through a hollow in the ground — the tail rises — the axle clatters over bumps — trees rush toward us — the clatter stops — the ground recedes — we are resting on the air — Up, past riggers and mechanics — over treetops — across a ravine, like a hawk — The ground unfolds — we bank — it tilts against a wing — a hidden, topsy-turvy stage with height to draw its curtain.

Trees become bushes; barns, toys; cows turn into rabbits as we climb. I lose all conscious connection with the past. I live only in the moment in this strange, unmortal space, crowded with beauty, pierced with danger. The horizon retreats, and veils itself in haze. The great, squared fields of Nebraska become patchwork on a planet's disk. All the country around Lincoln lies like a relief map below — its lake, its raveled bend of river, its capital, its offices and suburbs — a culture of men adhering to the medium of earth.

The world tilts again — another bank — we tighten in a spiral — My head is heavy — the seat presses hard against me — I become conscious of my body's weight, of the strength it takes to lift an arm — Fields curve around a wing tip — gravity is playing tag with space — Landing wires loosen — vibrate with the air. How can these routed wooden spars, how can that matchwork skeleton of ribs withstand such pressure?

> Those slender flying wires, hardly larger than an eagle's
> tendon — how can they bind fuselage to wings? On
> the farm we used more metal to tie a wagon to a horse!
> — Charles Lindbergh

The flying school was not, however, what Charles had
hoped. Not only was he the only student, but there was
only one teacher and he didn't like to fly. He had watched
his closest friend die in a crash and had been staying on the
ground as much as possible ever since.

Each time Charles showed up for his lesson, the instruc-
tor would have a reason they couldn't go up that day. By
May, an entire month later, he had flown only eight hours.
And when "Slim" (as the tall, slender budding pilot was
called) realized that Ray Page was about to sell the school's
only dual-control plane, he knew it was time to move on.

BARNSTORMING

In May 1922, Lindbergh approached Erold Bahl who was
about to take off barnstorming around parts of Nebraska,
Kansas, and Colorado. Bahl had just bought Ray Page's last
dual-control plane. He was precisely the kind of aviator
Lindbergh admired — a confident and extraordinarily skillful flyer, but one who refused to take unnecessary risks.
Unlike other pilots, who wore leather helmets and khaki
breeches (as did Lindbergh), Bahl wore an ordinary business
suit and simply turned his cap backward when he entered
the cockpit of his plane. He viewed aviation as a serious
profession and acted accordingly. He frowned on flyers who
took unnecessary risks, got themselves killed, and therefore

damaged the reputation of the fledgling business of aviation. He could, however, be daring when he thought the time was right. His sterling reputation was well-deserved: When Erold Bahl took a plane up, the mechanics came out of the hangar to watch.

Lindbergh asked Bahl if he could go along with him as an assistant. He would take care of the plane and help "work" the crowds. Lindbergh even offered to pay his own expenses — gaining experience meant that much to him. Bahl, who liked "Slim," agreed. And, after a while, Bahl began paying Lindbergh's expenses.

The first rule of barnstorming was attracting a crowd. This meant flying from pasture to pasture and field to field, landing the plane and convincing the curious and the courageous (many who had never seen a plane before) to take a ten-minute, five-dollar ride.

Lindbergh had an idea to help attract more people. His idea was simple: As they flew over a town, Lindbergh would stand on the wing of the plane and wave to the people below. Bahl agreed, and Lindbergh began his barnstorming days.

This poster was a typical broadside advertisement of the barnstorming days. Note the mention of Lindbergh.

After barnstorming with Bahl, Lindbergh watched a trick parachute-jumping exhibition at Ray Page's in mid-June put on by Charles Hardin and his wife, Kathryn. The Hardins made parachutes and drummed up business by staging these demonstrations. (This was a time when parachutes weren't in general use yet.) Lindbergh watched in complete fascination.

Hardin's specialty was to make multiple parachute drops during one descent to the ground. He claimed to be the only one in the world who did it. He accomplished this by having a number of chutes — sometimes as many as six — attached to each other so that they could be opened and then cut free as he fell to earth.

Lindbergh, who had never parachuted before, decided immediately that he wanted to try a double jump his first time out. Hardin was astonished but agreed, partly because Lindbergh implied that he might want to buy one of his $125 parachutes after the jump.

Lindbergh, who had already demonstrated his fearlessness wing-walking with Bahl, had a personal obstacle he felt driven to overcome.

At infrequent intervals through life I had dreamt of falling off some high roof or precipice. I'd felt terror and sickening fear as my body sank helplessly toward ground.

— Charles Lindbergh

At times the dreams were so bad he woke shaking, his body covered with a cold sweat. He wanted to end those boyhood nightmares once and for all. To do that, Lindbergh chose to do the thing he feared most: fall from a great height.

Displaying the will and determination that would — in the not-too-distant future — make him the most famous man in the world, Lindbergh prepared for the jump.

The next afternoon, when the plane reached 2,000 feet, he climbed out onto the right wing and, when the pilot gave him the signal, jumped.

The first chute opened properly and he cut it away with his knife, causing him to descend again in a rapid free fall. He braced himself, knowing that when the second chute opened, the harness would pull tight against his body. But the second chute failed to open.

Hardin, hurrying to get the chute ready for Lindbergh's first jump, had run out of the twine he usually used to tie the chutes together. He had substituted ordinary grocery string. The grocery string had broken, causing the second chute to delay in opening. Finally, after Lindbergh had fallen hundreds of feet, tumbling upside down, the second chute opened and he landed roughly on the ground.

Lindbergh, unshaken by the experience, and unaware of how close he had come to dying, said he felt fine.

The double jump instantly transformed Lindbergh from apprentice to respected equal. Veteran flyers were now willing to teach the young aviator the tricks of the trade.

Life changed after that jump. I noticed it in the attitude of those who came to help gather up my 'chute — in Hardin's acceptance of me as a brother parachutist, in Page's realization that I'd done what he didn't dare to do. I'd stepped suddenly to the highest level of daring. . . .

— Charles Lindbergh

Hardin taught Lindbergh many of the things he had learned: Always relax when landing; face the direction you were drifting toward when you land; in a strong wind, release the straps of your harness before you hit the ground to avoid the danger of being dragged along by the uncollapsed canopy.

And the nightmares vanished forever.

> . . . I've never fallen in my dreams since I actually fell through air. That factual experience seems to have removed completely some illogical, subconscious dread.
>
> — Charles Lindbergh

In July 1922, Lindbergh hooked up with Harold J. "Shorty" Lynch, who was taking off on a barnstorming tour. Lindbergh did triple duty as a wing-walker, parachute jumper, and mechanic. They toured together for four months in parts of Colorado, Wyoming, Kansas, and Montana. Lynch printed flyers proclaiming their star performer: *DAREDEVIL LINDBERGH.*

As they traveled to county fairs and homecoming events they were accompanied by a fox terrier who belonged to the plane's owner. The feisty dog insisted on riding with them. Lindbergh, afraid that their mascot might fall out, fashioned a harness that secured the dog to the cockpit and insured his safety.

Each day Lindbergh learned more about barnstorming. He learned to dangle from the underside of a plane by clenching a leather strap in his teeth. He learned to wing-walk while the plane looped the loop. And he learned how these things were done. You didn't really hang from a plane by your teeth — it just looked that way. In reality a cable attached to a shoulder harness inside your jacket kept you suspended in midair — a cable too thin to be seen from the ground. And the reason you didn't fall off the wing when the plane looped the loop was because four cables held you steady while your feet were anchored in steel cups attached to the wing.

But Lindbergh wanted to do the flying, not only the wing-walking, the tricks, and the double jumping.

In late April 1923, with money he had saved plus a bank loan cosigned by his father, he bought his first plane. It was a surplus World War I Curtiss JN-4D, or "Jenny" as it was known. He neglected to mention when he bought it that he had never flown a Jenny nor soloed in any plane. It took a week of takeoff and landing lessons before Lindbergh was able to go off on his own. He immediately proceeded to get lost, find himself in situations that resulted in forced landings and, a number of times, crack up the plane. But he was learning to fly.

The Jenny was light and maneuverable. That was the good news. Unfortunately, it was also slow and underpowered and had no brakes. A strong headwind or downdraft could mean trouble, especially on takeoff and when it came to clearing trees or wires. If the wind was strong enough the Jenny might not even get off the ground.

Undaunted, Lindbergh took off to barnstorm around the country in his new plane.

Forced to fly the underpowered Jenny, Lindbergh developed piloting skills good enough to compensate. Barnstorming on his own gave him the opportunity to add to his already extensive knowledge of engines, airplane design, and cockpit controls. Now he gained experience in judging field and weather conditions and making the life-or-

Lindbergh's first plane, the Jenny, after one of its many crack-ups.

death decisions essential to becoming a successful pilot.

He earned a reputation as an astonishing and fearless stunt flyer. He could do it all: spins, "the falling leaf," barrel rolls, and his specialty—climbing straight up, then diving straight down at top speed until it looked as if a crash was unavoidable and then, at the very last moment, pulling out. It was the motorcycle maneuver in the air.

He even took his mother barnstorming. For ten days they flew from town to town, flying in low to attract crowds to the pasture Charles chose as a landing field and center ring. Evangeline helped with everything: She threw leaflets over the side of the cockpit to announce their arrival, negotiated with the farmers for the use of their pastures, and sold tickets for rides with *DAREDEVIL LINDBERGH*. But barnstorming wasn't as lucrative as it once had been. There

were too many pilots and, at times, prices fell to a dollar or
two a ride. Even at that price it was difficult to find any tak-
ers. Too often Lindbergh would fly into town just after another gypsy flyer had left, leaving no business to be had. At
times Lindbergh was making so little money he took jobs as
a handyman (at $15 a week), a flying instructor, and a gas
station attendant.

CADET

That summer, 1923, Lindbergh started hearing about the
newer and more powerful planes being built. Barnstorming
was okay if all you ever wanted to fly was a Jenny. But the
only place to fly the newer planes was the United States
Army. The prospect of further testing his flying skills greatly
interested the young pilot. He wanted to be a first-class
pilot and the word was that the Army was the only place to
get that kind of training. He was so eager that he wrote to
Washington for an application at once. He took the exam,
and on March 15, 1924, enrolled as a cadet in the Army Air
Service Cadet Program in San Antonio, Texas.

Lindbergh was immediately confronted with an unexpected challenge. Afternoons were not spent flying or working
on planes. They were spent in the classroom — historically
alien territory for him. He was required to study twenty-
five subjects in ground-school. If you failed three, you
"washed out."

Previously, classroom studies had been enough to cause
Lindbergh's attention to wander. But not this time. He
knew he wanted what the Army had to offer, and he disci-
plined himself to study.

Second Lieutenant Lindbergh in uniform, March 1925.

. . . [At] the Army flying school in Texas . . . I'd really
gotten down to business, worked on my studies as I'd
never worked before. I hadn't been much impressed by
university diplomas. They seemed advantageous but
unessential bits of paper, not worth the sacrifices their
award required. But an Air Service pilot's wings were
like a silver passport to the realm of light.

— Charles Lindbergh

In fact, the courses were so difficult that Lindbergh, always someone who could rise to the challenge if he wanted
to, gave it all he had. Weekends and evenings found him
diligently doing his homework. Within months he had
learned things about aerodynamics, meteorology, radio
communication, and other technical and mechanical aspects
of flying that would have been impossible to grasp if he'd
continued barnstorming around the country in the Jenny.

He also became a member of the Caterpillar Club. Membership was awarded to anyone making an emergency exit
via parachute from a plane in flight. (Parachutes were made
of silk, and silk was spun by caterpillars, hence the name.)
Lindbergh's class was the first to be issued parachutes. No
longer afraid of falling, Lindbergh survived four jumps by
using a parachute — more than anyone else. The first one,
amazingly enough, enabled him to survive a midair colli-
sion. It was the first time anyone had done that.

Only 18 of the 104 cadets who began training graduated.
Second Lieutenant Lindbergh graduated at the top of his
class.

In Texas, Lindbergh's reputation as a premier pilot grew.
So did his reputation as a merciless practical joker. He sub-

jected his classmates to a wide variety of "pranks," some more dangerous than humorous.

He positioned a bucket of cold water over a door so that his victim would get soaked when he entered. Cadets sleeping with their mouths open awoke abruptly to a face filled with shaving cream. He put grasshoppers in the bed of a fellow cadet who was deathly afraid of being bitten by scorpions, and used frogs, lizards, skunks, and even poisonous snakes as part of his seemingly endless repertoire.

One "practical joke," pulled off after he was a cadet, almost ended tragically. Bud Gurney, whom Lindbergh knew from his days in Lincoln, came home from a night of hard drinking. Thirsty, he reached for a jug of ice water, but Lindbergh had replaced the ice water with kerosene. Gurney was rushed to the hospital, where his badly burned stomach and throat were treated.

AIRMAIL

Airmail service in the United States began in 1918. Within two years a transcontinental route was operating between New York and San Francisco.

There were serious problems, however. The planes were poorly designed for the jobs they were doing. There was no radio communication between the pilot and ground operations. Pilots nicknamed the planes "flaming coffins" because the fuel tanks, which were situated between the cockpit and the engine, too often exploded during forced landings. Fog, sleet, snow, and early darkness in winter added to the danger. Pilots were frequently forced to make emergency landings in rugged terrain. Even official landing fields were not properly lighted. Frigid temperatures caused equipment to fail, and weather reports were so unreliable that most pilots made their decisions based on local weather conditions: weather they could actually see. But that meant they took their chances with the weather that was minutes, hours, and miles down the line. If forced to land, they were instructed to get the mail to the nearest train. Flying the mail was the most dangerous job in America, and the numbers told the story. Thirty-one of the first forty pilots hired were killed in crashes.

By 1925 the government decided to turn the operation over to private companies who would bid on the feeder lines that connected cities like St. Louis and Chicago. The exclusive rights to that route were awarded to the St. Louis-based Robertson Aircraft Company.

The Robertson brothers had been impressed when they met Charles Lindbergh at an international air race. Lindbergh had gone to St. Louis after graduating from the Army Air Service Training School. Living in a boardinghouse and making St. Louis's Lambert Field his base of operations, he did anything he could that would make him money while allowing him to fly. He instructed students, did some test flying, and barnstormed. One night he even flew with fireworks attached to his wings.

By now Lindbergh was considered one of the most skillful aviators in the country. He was blessed with extraordinary physical attributes: extremely good vision, above average muscular coordination, and excellent health. To this he added sharp mental focus. Once in the air there was nothing that Lindbergh couldn't do. He was unflappable in the face of unexpected and immediate danger. Those familiar with flying were equally impressed with how meticulously he went about his flight preparations.

Lindbergh's reputation, along with the Robertson brothers' personal observations of his skills, won him the job as Chief Pilot in charge of the St. Louis-Chicago airmail route. He was responsible for nearly everything. He hired the two other pilots, rented the necessary equipment, and plotted the landing fields and the routes.

Lindbergh's first flight from Chicago to St. Louis was on April 26, 1926. He flew in an open, twin-cockpit plane with the airmail sack in the sealed forward cockpit. He and his two pilots flew five round-trips a week, establishing a remarkable record for reliability despite the problems and dangers. And even when forced down, Lindbergh would fly as long as he could in order to empty his tanks. He did this

Lindbergh loads mailbags before taking off on his first flight as an airmail pilot.

so that the mail would not be burned in an explosion when he landed. He learned other tricks, too. When forced to parachute from a plane in darkness or fog, he crossed his legs in order to avoid straddling electrical wires, and protected his face with his hands upon landing.

Once he parachuted from a plane only to find himself close to being killed by the plane he had abandoned. When the engine had stopped, Lindbergh figured it was out of gas. But the steep descent must have sent more gas into the carburetor, and the propeller was going full speed. Lindbergh had neglected to turn off the engine. The plane spiraled down, narrowly missing with each spiral the parachuting Lindbergh. Agile and resourceful as always, he escaped with only a dislocated shoulder caused by a rough landing.

Chapter Three

THE SPIRIT OF ST. LOUIS

*I had been attracted to aviation by its adventure, not its
safety, by the love of wind and height and wings. It was the
love of flying primarily, and secondarily the hope of
advancing aviation's development, that caused me to make
the New York-to-Paris flight with my* Spirit of St. Louis *in
1927.*

— Charles Lindbergh

In the fall of 1926 Charles Lindbergh watched newsreels at
a movie theater reporting on René Fonck's preparations for
his transatlantic flight. Some of the world's premier pilots
were planning to compete for the $25,000 Orteig prize.

While flying the mail, Lindbergh thought about the flight.

. . . I envisioned a nonstop flight between New York
and Paris across the Atlantic. I believed that airplanes

and engines had advanced to a point where such a
flight was practicable, and I was convinced that the
broad experience I had gained as a civil and military
pilot put me in a good position to organize and exe-
cute it. It would be an extraordinary adventure and, if
successful, help to advance the cause of aviation, to
which I was devoted.

— Charles Lindbergh

He had been flying constantly for the past four years,
often at night and, at times, in the worst winter weather
conditions. He believed he could do it. He could win the
Orteig prize.

Why shouldn't I fly from New York to Paris? I'm almost twenty-five. I have more than four years of aviation behind me, and close to two thousand hours in
the air. I've barnstormed over half of the forty-eight
States. I've flown my mail through the worst of
nights. . . . During my year . . . as a flying cadet, I
learned the basic elements of navigation. . . . Why am
I not qualified for such a flight?

Not so long ago, when I was a student in college,
just flying an airplane seemed a dream. But that dream
turned into reality. Then, as a two-hundred-hour pilot
barnstorming through the country for a living, the
wings of the Army Air Service seemed almost beyond
reach. But I won them. Finally, to be a pilot of the
night mail appeared the summit of ambition for a flyer;
yet here I am, in the cockpit of a mail plane boring
through the night. Why wouldn't a flight across the

ocean prove as possible as all these things have been? As I attempted them, I can — I will attempt that too. I'll organize a flight to Paris!

— Charles Lindbergh

He needed two things: the right plan and the right plane.

THE PLAN

ST. LOUIS–NEW YORK–PARIS FLIGHT

ACTION

1. Plan
2. Propaganda
3. Backers
4. Equipment
5. Co-operation of manufacturers
6. Accessory information
7. Point of departure
8. Advertising

ADVANTAGES

1. Revive St. Louis interest in aviation
2. Advertise St. Louis as an aviation city
3. Aid in making America first in the air
4. Promote nation-wide interest in aeronautics
5. Demonstrate perfection of modern equipment

RESULTS

1. Successful completion, winning $25,000 prize to cover expense
2. Complete failure

CO-OPERATION

1. Plane manufacturers
2. Motor manufacturers
3. Weather Department
4. State Department
5. Newspapers
6. Steamships

EQUIPMENT

1. Raft (sail)
2. Rockets
3. Clothing (waterproof)
4. Condensed food
5. Still (water)

MAPS

1. Prevailing winds
2. Coast and interior
3. Islands
4. Steamship travel

LANDMARKS

1. Islands
2. List of coast towns
3. Index of towns
4. Characteristic names
5. Characteristic terrain

— Charles Lindbergh

THE PLANE

Lindbergh approached a number of St. Louis businessmen in hopes that his local reputation would at least get him a hearing. It did, and more. His key support came from Harry Knight, a broker and president of the St. Louis Flying Club. Lindbergh had recently begun giving Knight flying lessons.

Knight set up a meeting with Harold Bixby, who was the head of the St. Louis Chamber of Commerce and had recently bought his own plane. Lindbergh presented his proposal, which stressed the opportunity for the city of St. Louis. Centrally located, St. Louis already had one of the best commercial airports in the country. Sponsoring a successful, historic, transatlantic flight might allow St. Louis to lead the United States into what Lindbergh believed was the bright future of commercial aviation. Knight, Bixby, and other St. Louis businessmen were impressed with Lindbergh's confidence and his vision. They agreed to sponsor the flight.

A $15,000 budget was eventually established ($2,000 of which came from money Lindbergh had saved barnstorming and flying the mail) and a name: the *Spirit of St. Louis.*

Much to their credit, Lindbergh's backers offered their support, no strings attached. Lindbergh was to choose the plane and decide on all other aspects of the proposed flight. Their confidence in him never wavered, despite the radical nature of his plan.

Lindbergh seriously questioned the prevailing wisdom that flying multiengine planes was safer than flying single-engine planes. He believed multiple engines increased, rather than decreased, the possibilities of failure. He doubted what others accepted — that if one engine failed the others would keep the plane in the air.

According to Lindbergh, a single-engine plane, flown by a lone pilot, had the best chance for success. The less weight, the more fuel, the greater the range. This theory also flew in the face of conventional wisdom, which said that the very least you needed was a crew of two: a pilot and a navigator. Flying solo across the Atlantic was simply suicide. The burden on the pilot was considered too great — he would have to stay awake for over thirty hours, enduring constant stresses. It couldn't be done, the experts said.

Lindbergh disagreed.

. . . I'm not sure three engines would really add much to safety on a flight like that . . . the plane would be overloaded with fuel anyway. There'd be three times the chance of engine failure; and if one of them stopped over the ocean, you probably couldn't get back to land with the other two. A multiengined plane is awfully big and heavy . . . Fonck had three engines, but that didn't help him any when his landing gear

gave way. A single-engined plane might even be safer,
everything considered.

— Charles Lindbergh

He immediately began searching for the right plane and
someone who would be willing to sell it to him for the
right price. He contacted a number of aircraft companies.
Some didn't respond and some turned him down. They
didn't want to build a single-engine plane for a transatlantic
flight — an idea they considered foolish. And, besides,
Lindbergh was relatively unknown when compared to in-
ternationally known aviators like Byrd, Fonck, Davis,
Chamberlin, and Nungesser.

Time was running out. Indeed, it might have already run
out. By early 1927, American and French aviators, some
with unlimited financial backing, were already preparing
their flights. Lindbergh was determined to find a plane and
find it now.

He had a plane in mind and arranged a meeting with the
plane's designer, and later, the plane's owner.

After a number of meetings and telegrams back and
forth, Lindbergh advised his St. Louis backers that the
owner was willing to sell the plane for $15,000. This was a
high price for just the plane — it left nothing for purchasing
the engine, running tests, and other expenses. But Lindbergh's supporters, displaying the confidence they had in
the young flyer, handed him a check for the full amount
and advised him to return to New York and close the deal.

. . . I'm staring at the . . . figures on a slip of paper in
my hand — FIFTEEN THOUSAND DOLLARS . . .

"Pay to the order of Charles A. Lindbergh" it says on the back. . . . "I didn't know you were going to make this out to me personally," I say.

Bixby laughs. "Well Slim, Harry and I decided that if we couldn't trust you with a check, we ought not to take part in the project at all."

"When do you plan on starting back to New York?" Knight asks.

"I'll take the train this afternoon," I tell him.

— Charles Lindbergh

But when Lindbergh arrived in New York he was surprised to hear, for the first time, that although the owner would indeed sell them the plane, he insisted on choosing the pilot.

"I'm afraid there's been a misunderstanding," I say. "We wouldn't be interested in such an arrangement. This is a St. Louis project. We'd naturally want to work with you very closely in running tests and planning the flight; but if we buy the plane, we're going to control it, and we'll pick our own crew."

— Charles Lindbergh

The owner suggested Lindbergh think it over and call him in the morning. When he did, the owner asked him if he had changed his mind. Lindbergh hung up the phone. He had wasted his time, and time was not on Lindbergh's side.

But destiny was.

In early February 1927 (during the time he was negotiating to buy the plane in New York), the Ryan Airlines Corporation of San Diego, California, had responded within twenty-four hours of receiving Lindbergh's telegram regarding a plane for his proposed transatlantic flight.

Yes, they could produce a plane that could fly nonstop, New York to Paris. It would cost $6,000 (not including engine) and would take three months to build.

Lindbergh traveled to San Diego to meet the people at Ryan and see their facilities. He was impressed, and the visit convinced him that they could give him what he needed.

Lindbergh had been fortunate in finding his financial backers. They provided not only money but the kind of support that had put the project on the right track — a track it was to stay on from the beginning to the end. And now, he was equally fortunate in finding Ryan Airlines. Although the company was small (their plant had been a fish cannery), the management was knowledgeable and professional. Their workers appeared to be capable and skilled at their craft, and Lindbergh believed they were willing to dedicate themselves to delivering a superior plane. And a superior plane was just what Lindbergh, the superior pilot, had in mind.

In late February 1927, after a formal agreement was reached, everyone at Ryan turned their full attention to building the *Spirit of St. Louis* in record time.

Chief engineer Donald Hall worked, at times, thirty-six hours at a stretch, often arriving at five A.M. so he could review what had been done the day before. Work on other planes nearly stopped. Ryan workers, sensing that they were participating in something special, worked morning, noon, and night, seven days a week. Voluntary overtime became normal operating procedure. Meals were eaten when and where they could be squeezed in. Hall, Lindbergh, and Frank Mahoney, the company's president, decided to modify an existing Ryan model by, among other things, outfit-

Building the Spirit of St. Louis. *Here the wing is being taken out of the Ryan plant and lowered to the ground as Lindbergh, in a dark suit (top right corner), supervises.*

ting the plane with extra fuel tanks and increasing the wing area. This would give the plane a maximum range of 4,000 miles, more than enough to reach Paris.

In fact neither Hall nor Lindbergh knew *precisely* the distance from New York to Paris:

"It's going to be something like forty hours in the air, you know. Say, exactly how far is it between New York and Paris by the route you're going to follow?"

"It's about 3,500 miles. We could get a pretty close check by scaling it off a globe. Do you know where there is one?"

"There's a globe at the public library. It only takes a few minutes to drive there. I've got to know what the distance is before I can make any accurate calculations. My car's right outside."

We climb into a rusting, black Buick roadster and head downtown.

"It's 3,600 statute miles."

— Charles Lindbergh

Hall and Lindbergh worked side by side making the final design decisions. Lindbergh insisted that the main fuel tank be placed in front of the pilot's seat rather than behind as usual. This way, he would not be caught between the engine and an exploding gas tank in case of a forced landing. Lindbergh was keenly aware that too many pilots had died because of that. This arrangement, however, meant that the main fuel tanks would block his forward vision.

"But then you couldn't see straight ahead," [Hall] argues. "The tanks would be directly in front of you. I

This cutaway diagram shows how the main fuel tank in the front of the Spirit of St. Louis *blocks Lindbergh's forward vision. Designed to fit Lindbergh perfectly, the plane utilizes every inch of space.*

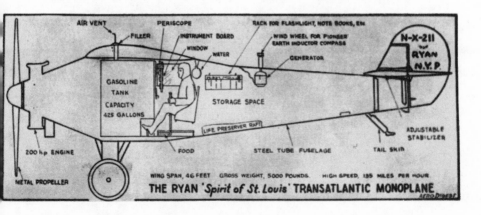

thought you would want to sit behind the engine so as to have the best possible vision."

"You know we always look out at an angle when we take off," I tell him. "The nose of the fuselage blocks out the field straight ahead, anyway. Some of the mail pilots even have their windshield painted black to cut down reflection at night. I don't need straight forward vision . . ."

"I'm not referring to take-off," Hall says. "I know the engine blocks out forward vision like a barn door while the airplane is in a high angle of attack altitude — I've done a little piloting myself. I'm thinking of forward vision in normal flight."

"There's not much need to see ahead in normal flight," I reply. "I won't be following any airways. When I'm near a flying field, I can watch the sky ahead by making shallow banks. Why don't we leave the cockpit in the rear, and fair it in? All I need is a window on each side to see through. The top of the fuselage could be the top of the cockpit. A cockpit like that wouldn't add any resistance at all. I think we ought to give first consideration to efficiency in flight; second, to protection in a crack-up; third, to pilot comfort. I don't see why a cockpit in the rear doesn't cover all three. Besides, I don't like the idea of being sandwiched in between the engine and a gas tank the way you are up forward. If you crack up you haven't got a chance in a place like that."

— Charles Lindbergh

Range and fuel efficiency were of paramount importance. Therefore weight — what to take and what not to take — became an ongoing, critical decision. Lindbergh was adamant about not taking anything he considered unnecessary. He refused to take a radio because it would be heavy and unreliable, especially in bad weather when it would be needed most. A parachute was out because it weighed twenty pounds, and it would only be of use flying over land. Most of the time Lindbergh would be over water, and in the frigid North Atlantic a parachute would not help. Navigation lights, a sextant, and gas gauges were discarded. He would keep track of fuel consumption by using his watch. He would navigate by dead reckoning, using his maps and visual checks of the terrain below: rocky coast, a winding river, railroad tracks, etc.

He designed his own boots, which were lighter than reg-

The cramped cockpit of the Spirit of St. Louis. *During the flight, Lindbergh would sit in the small wicker chair for 33½ hours.*

"We Built the Ryan New York to Paris Plane."

Workers at the Ryan plant stand proudly in front of the Spirit of St. Louis. *Lindbergh is seventh from the left.*

ular flying boots, and he cut unnecessary portions from his maps, saving further precious ounces.

He did take what he considered sensible: an inflatable rubber raft, a hunting knife, a ball of string, two fishhooks, a large needle, a small flashlight, matches, and a hacksaw blade.

His instrument panel included: a speed and drift indicator, an airspeed indicator, a tachometer, an altimeter and an oil pressure gauge, an earth inductor compass, bank and turn indicators, a temperature gauge, and a clock. There was a cut-down wicker chair for him to sit on.

In late April 1927, after sixty days of intense effort, the tiny, shiny, silver *Spirit of St. Louis* was ready.

It was only 9 feet 8 inches high, just under 28 feet long and had a 46-foot wingspan. It was driven by a reliable 220-horsepower, air-cooled, nine-cylinder Wright J-5C "Whirlwind" engine. The engine had been carefully inspected by the Wright Aeronautical Corporation (originally founded by the Wright brothers) and provided with a special mechanism to keep it greased during the flight. The company estimated that it could run 9,000 hours without breaking down. The empty plane weighed a little over 2,000 pounds, 5,200 pounds when gasoline was added. It was a highly efficient airplane.

Only a few weeks before, it had looked as if Lindbergh would never get his chance. Surely one of his famous competitors would take off before his plane could be readied. But things had not turned out as expected. Fonck and Byrd's planes had cracked up and they'd experienced, along with Chamberlin, subsequent problems delaying their flights. Davis and Wooster had died the day the *Spirit of St. Louis* was completed.

On May 8, 1927, came further news, as radio stations

One of the most famous photographs of Lindbergh with his newly finished plane.

interrupted their normal programming with bulletins. Nungesser and Coli had taken off from Paris and had been spotted over the Atlantic. They were due in New York the next day, where crowds were already gathering. But the sightings were false. Nungesser and Coli were never heard from again.

On May 10, 1927, Charles Lindbergh, piloting the *Spirit of St. Louis,* took off from San Diego headed for St. Louis, en route to New York and Paris. Lindbergh set records for the San Diego–St. Louis leg and, on May 12, 1927, landed at Curtiss Field, Long Island, setting a record for the fastest transcontinental flight.

Chapter Four

$\mathscr{A}$ I R B O R N E

The danger and daring of such a feat are highlighted by the fact that to this day no one else has flown alone, nonstop, from New York to Paris in a single-engine plane . . . it popularized, even revolutionized aviation like no other single event before or since, with the possible exception of the pioneering flight of the Wright brothers.
                                    — Joshua Stoff, aviation historian

ARRIVAL

Almost as soon as my plane comes to a stop it's sur-rounded by newspaper photographers. I shout at them to keep clear of the propeller, but no one pays atten-tion. Two men are trying to get a picture of me in the cockpit. Others are in front, at the sides, and behind the plane. Heavy motion-picture cameras on their

55

tripods are pointing at me. I've never seen such excitement and disorder around aircraft . . .

There's a milling about as I climb down from my cockpit. Several men are making notes on pads of paper. They must be reporters. Space is cleared with difficulty, and I take position, as requested, with one hand on the propeller of the *Spirit of St. Louis.*

Each moment I feel more uncomfortable. It's not like San Diego or St. Louis. These cameramen curse and jostle one another for position, while they take pictures from every conceivable angle. Some stand up, others kneel or crouch; a few even lie on the ground to point their lenses at me. They take photographs head on, photographs from the quarter, photographs from the side, distant shots, close-ups, motion pictures, and stills.

"Smile!"

"Look this way, will ya?"

"Shake hands with somebody."

"Say something."

. . .

They must have enough pictures to last forever. I start to leave.

"Wait a minute. Gotta get a close-up."

"Hold it."

"Just one more."

They crowd nearer. Cameras come within three or four feet of my face. I turn away and begin walking toward the nearest hangar. Photographers run in front. Reporters close in around me; there must be a dozen of them.

"When're you going to start for Paris?"

"Tell us something about your flight from California."

"Did you have any close calls?"

. . .

"What does yer mother say about all this?"

There's no use asking the questions because I don't get a chance to answer any of them. Somebody slaps me on the back, hard. Somebody else pulls sideways on my arm.

— Charles Lindbergh

When Charles Lindbergh arrived in the New York City area he was no longer an unknown. His new transcontinental record, breaking the one set four years earlier, was responsible for some of the notoriety, but that was only part of the story.

He arrived from the West Coast, flying alone in his spartan plane, which seemed too small for such a large undertaking. He appeared on the scene the all-American hero; the underdog, going up against famous aviators supported by powerful financial groups, piloting huge, elaborately equipped multiengined planes.

He knew that he was as good as any pilot in the business . . . (he was) an unknown kid, swooping out of the sky to challenge the greatest flyers in the world — and making them admit that perhaps he had the stuff it took to make his challenge stick.

— Harry Bruno, Lindbergh's public relations advisor

The young, sandy-haired, blue-eyed photogenic pilot with the charming smile was beginning to attract crowds

The all-American hero in flying gear.

wherever he went. Thirty thousand people gathered to see him and the other pilots the first Sunday after his arrival. They reached out to touch him whenever they could. A rope and two policemen were needed to keep the crowds away from the hangar where the *Spirit of St. Louis* was being readied. One night, when the hangar door was opened to allow a truck to enter, the police struggled to stop the crowd from rushing in. The roof of a shed collapsed because so many people had positioned themselves there, hoping to get a glimpse of the plane or its brave, bashful pilot. Teenage girls treated Lindbergh like a Hollywood movie star. His natural shyness just made him more attractive, both to the adoring public and the press — ever eager for a good story.

Reporters, sent by sensation-seeking newspapers, hounded him, calling him "The Lone Eagle," "The Flyin' Fool," "The Flyin' Kid," and "Lucky Lindy." Lindbergh disliked all of these nicknames, but especially the last. He believed in sound engineering, proper training, constant diligence, and hard work — not luck. He valued good public relations, but took flying too seriously to enjoy being treated by the reporters in a manner that showed they had no respect for the enormous challenge he was taking on.

He was repulsed by their rude behavior, constant badgering, and inaccurate reporting.

Contacts with the press became increasingly distasteful to me. I felt that interviews and photographs tended to confuse and cheapen life, especially those printed in the "tabloid" papers.

— Charles Lindbergh

Lindbergh was aggravated by eager press photographers who often crowded the field, making it difficult for him to land safely.

At times he tried to be obliging. He had his picture taken with his rivals, Byrd, Chamberlin, and Fonck; he cooperated with the photographers by posing while checking the plane's engine. But whatever he did never seemed to be enough. The photographers always wanted one more shot, shoving cameras in his face and even lying on the ground to get a picture of him walking. Reporters asked one irrelevant question after another, such as, What kind of girls do you like? or What's your favorite pie? Rarely a question about aviation. Once, photographers swarmed onto the field when he was trying to land after a test flight. Planes, at that time, were difficult to maneuver and had no brakes. Lindbergh damaged the plane when he swerved to avoid injuring or killing someone. He was further angered that photographers not only got the shot they wanted but that the story was reported as if the accident were *his* fault.

One night photographers burst into his hotel room and took pictures of him in his pajamas. They had to be physically escorted into the hall. He had even come to believe they were waiting and hoping that he or one of the other pilots would crash.

He refused to answer their many questions about his mother. But that didn't stop them. They tracked her down in Detroit, where she had returned to teach high school. His father had died of a brain tumor three years earlier. She, too, was hounded by the media and besieged by curiosity seekers. Reporters called her on the phone and came right to the door. They asked her if she realized how dangerous the flight was. Did she know how many experienced pilots had already died in the attempt? The normally calm Evangeline became worried and went to New York to see her son. Charles was angered by the insensitivity of the media. When she arrived he took her inside the hangar so they could have some privacy. When they emerged the photographers asked them to embrace. Charles refused. One newspaper faked the photograph anyway (a common practice by the tabloid newspapers of the time) — putting Charles's and Evangeline's faces on the bodies of two other people who had posed kissing each other.

I was furious . . . My mother had come to New York to be with me for a few hours before I started out for Paris. We had posed together for the photographers, but refused to take the maudlin positions some of them had asked for. The next day I was startled to see newspaper photographs showing us in exactly those positions. I

Lindbergh and his mother oblige the press by posing in front of the Spirit of St. Louis.

thought it cheaply sentimental and thoroughly dishonest on the part of the papers. At New York I began to realize how much irresponsibility and license can lurk behind the shining mask called freedom of the press. . . .
— Charles Lindbergh

THE COAST IS CLEAR

All the while Lindbergh, along with Byrd and Chamberlin, waited for the weather to improve. He had been waiting for almost a week. The weather had been bad since mid-April: fog near Newfoundland and Nova Scotia, while in New York the rain fell and skies remained threatening. The weather report continued to forecast precipitation and fog.

Lindbergh agreed to take a break from the strain of waiting and weather-watching. He and a group of men associated with the flight (representatives of the engine, gasoline, oil, and instrumentation companies) headed for New York City to see a Broadway musical. The city was shrouded in mist from the light rain. They decided, just in case, to check to see if there had been any change in the forecast. Unexpectedly, there was. A high pressure system had moved in, and the weather over the Atlantic was clearing.

Lindbergh believed that if he waited any longer Byrd or Chamberlin would surely take off. He decided to turn around, head back to Long Island, and prepare to take off at dawn. On the way, over dinner, he outlined the plans. The preliminary fueling had to be taken care of, a full inspection done, the police notified to control the crowds, and the plane moved from Curtiss to Roosevelt Field. The runway at Curtiss was too short. Roosevelt Field, which was right next to it, had a runway that had been recently lengthened by Commander Byrd. Byrd, who had spent a good deal of money on this improvement, had exclusive use of Roosevelt Field. However, in a show of the professionalism that had characterized the competition for the Orteig prize, he offered to let Lindbergh use the runway.

In the morning the *Spirit of St. Louis* would be moved to Roosevelt Field. Until then, Lindbergh would try to get some sleep. It was a little before midnight. He was to be awakened at 2:30 A.M. A couple of hours sleep was all he would get. But the reporters would see to it that he wouldn't even get that.

Somehow they had gotten word of Lindbergh's plans. *Their* plans included staying up all night and playing poker in the same hotel Lindbergh was staying at. The noise kept him up all night. In the early morning hours, preparing to go, he didn't feel tired — yet. He wondered if the lack of sleep would come to haunt him.

Two motorcycle policemen led the way. The *Spirit of St. Louis* was towed, tail first, by truck, across a rutty road to Roosevelt Field. A blanket protected the plane's engine from the mist. Lindbergh examined the field carefully, thinking about his plane, filled to capacity with gas, and the telephone wires he would have to clear.

One of the last photographs taken of Lindbergh before he set off for Paris.

As if the rain and muddy field weren't enough, the wind had shifted and now, rather than having a helpful tailwind, he would have to fight a headwind.

A reporter, noticing Lindbergh's bag of sandwiches, wondered aloud if that was all he was bringing. Lindbergh replied: "Wu-ll, if I get to Paris I won't need any more food, and if I don't, I won't need any either."

He put on his flight helmet, lowered his goggles, gave the signal to start the propeller and release the wheel chocks, opened the engine full-throttle, and guided the plane down the muddy runway as workers pushed and three men with fire extinguishers followed in a car. The *Spirit of St. Louis* labored to extricate itself from the muddy runway, passed the point of no return, lifted off, cleared the wires by twenty feet, and was airborne, headed for Paris.

It was 7:52 A.M., May 20, 1927.

Chapter Five

$\mathcal{A}$ L O N E

NEW YORK TO PARIS
MAY 20–21, 1927

GREEN GRASS . . . BELOW . . . PEOPLE LOOKING UP. . . . THE PLANE'S CLIMBING FASTER. . . . PLENTY OF HEIGHT, PLENTY OF POWER . . . I MUST GET A CHECK ON THE COMPASSES, WATCH FOR LANDMARKS, MAKE SURE THAT THE PLACES I FLY OVER ON THE EARTH'S SURFACE CORRESPOND TO THE SYMBOLS CROSSED BY THE BLACK-INKED LINE ON MY MAP. . . . BY FLYING CLOSE TO THE GROUND, I CAN SEE FARTHER THROUGH THE HAZE. THE *SPIRIT OF ST. LOUIS* . . . SEEMS TO FORM AN EXTENSION OF MY OWN BODY, READY TO FOLLOW MY WISH AS THE HAND FOLLOWS THE MIND'S DESIRE — INSTINCTIVELY, WITHOUT COMMANDING. . . . A NEWSPAPER

PLANE BANKS STEEPLY AND HEADS BACK . . . CAMERAS STICK-
ING OUT OF THE COCKPITS AND CABIN WINDOWS. . . . I WISH
THEY'D ALL GO AWAY. . . . I RELAX IN MY COCKPIT . . . I CAN
PRESS BOTH SIDES OF THE FUSELAGE WITH PARTLY OUT-
STRETCHED ELBOWS. THE INSTRUMENT BOARD IS AN EASY
REACH FORWARD FOR MY HAND, AND A THIN RIB ON THE
ROOF IS HOLLOWED SLIGHTLY TO LEAVE CLEARANCE FOR MY
HELMET. THERE'S ROOM ENOUGH, NO MORE, NO LESS; MY
COCKPIT HAS BEEN TAILORED TO ME LIKE A SUIT OF
CLOTHES . . . I MUSTN'T BE TOO DISAPPOINTED IF I HAVE TO
TURN BACK. I'VE NEVER COUNTED ON REACHING PARIS ON
THE FIRST TRY. I PLANNED ON STARTING SEVERAL TIMES IF
NEED BE.

THE THIRD HOUR: *Over the Atlantic*

RAPIDLY FADING OUT OF SIGHT BEHIND ME IS THE COAST
LINE OF THE UNITED STATES . . . I'M . . . HEADING OUT TO
SEA. . . . THE FIRST REAL TEST OF NAVIGATION IS AT HAND.
FOR MORE THAN TWO HOURS, I'LL BE OUT OF SIGHT OF
LAND. THERE'LL BE NO RIVERS OR CITIES WITH WHICH TO
CHECK MY COURSE . . . I NOSE DOWN CLOSER TO THE LOW,
ROLLING WAVES — A HUNDRED FEET — FIFTY FEET —
TWENTY FEET ABOVE THEIR SHIFTING SURFACES.

THE FOURTH HOUR: *Over the Atlantic*

I'M A LITTLE TIRED. THE SUN BEATING IN THROUGH THE
WINDOW OVERHEAD MAKES THE COCKPIT UNCOMFORTABLY
HOT. SHALL I TAKE OFF MY BLANKET-LINED FLIGHT SUIT? I
CAN WRIGGLE OUT WITHOUT TOO MUCH TROUBLE; BUT TO
PUT IT ON AGAIN WHILE I'M PILOTING WOULD BE A TREMEN-

DOUS EFFORT, AND I'LL SURELY NEED ITS WARMTH TONIGHT. WELL, I CAN AT LEAST PULL DOWN THE ZIPPER AND GET SOME COOL AIR AROUND MY CHEST. WHY DIDN'T I THINK OF THAT BEFORE? MY LEGS ARE STIFF AND CRAMPED. BUT THAT WON'T LAST MORE THAN THREE OR FOUR HOURS. THE DULL ACHE WILL GET WORSE FOR A TIME, AND THEN GO AWAY ALTOGETHER. I'VE EXPERIENCED THE FEELING BEFORE. IT BEGINS AFTER ABOUT THREE HOURS OF FLYING, AND ENDS AT ABOUT SEVEN . . . I'M HALF ASLEEP! I CUP MY HAND INTO THE SLIPSTREAM AND DEFLECT FRESH AIR AGAINST MY FACE. CHECK THE INSTRUMENTS — THAT WILL HELP.

THE FIFTH HOUR: *Over Nova Scotia*

IT'S NOON OF THE FIRST DAY. FOUR HUNDRED MILES FROM NEW YORK. THREE THOUSAND TWO HUNDRED MILES TO PARIS . . . LAND AHEAD! . . . NOVA SCOTIA . . . I FORGET ABOUT BEING TIRED. HERE'S A VITAL POINT IN THE FLIGHT. HOW ACCURATELY HAVE I HELD MY COURSE? . . . UNCONSCIOUSLY MY EYES ARE ALWAYS SEARCHING FOR THE PLACE I'D CHOOSE TO LAND SHOULD FAILURE COME AT THIS PARTICULAR MOMENT . . . I STUDY THE GROUND.

THE EIGHTH HOUR: *Over Nova Scotia*

FOG! I'M FLYING ALONG DREAMILY WHEN I SEE IT — A NARROW WHITE BAND ON THE HORIZON TO MY RIGHT . . . FOG — THE MOST DREADED OF ALL ENEMIES OF FLIGHT . . . IF THE FOG WILL ONLY HOLD OFF A FEW HOURS MORE, IF I CAN ONLY CHECK MY COURSE OVER NEWFOUNDLAND, IT WON'T MATTER WHAT HAPPENS AFTER THAT. I'LL ASK FOR NOTHING MORE UNTIL I REACH THE OTHER SIDE OF THE

OCEAN. THE 1,900 MILES OF WATER CAN BE COVERED WITH FOG — I'LL FLY ABOVE IT, OR UNDER IT, OR IN IT. NOTHING ELSE WILL MATTER IF THE COAST OF NEWFOUNDLAND IS CLEAR . . . MY COCKPIT IS SMALL, AND ITS WALLS ARE THIN; BUT INSIDE THIS COCOON I FEEL SECURE, DESPITE THE SPECULATIONS OF MY MIND . . . HERE ARE NO UNNECESSARY EXTRAS, ONLY THE BAREST ESSENTIALS OF LIFE AND FLIGHT. THERE ARE NO LETTERS TO GET OFF IN THE NEXT MAIL, NO TELEPHONE BELLS TO RING, NO LOOSE ODDS AND ENDS TO ATTEND TO IN SOME ADJOINING ROOM. THE FEW FURNISHINGS ARE WITHIN ARM'S LENGTH, AND ALL IN ORDER. A CABIN THAT FLIES THROUGH THE AIR, THAT'S WHAT I LIVE IN . . .

THE NINTH HOUR: *Over the Atlantic*

I'VE BEEN FLYING OVER LAND FOR MOST OF FOUR HOURS. THE SEA IS AS WELCOME A CHANGE AS THE COAST OF NOVA SCOTIA WAS . . . I NOSE THE *SPIRIT OF ST. LOUIS* DOWN TO MEET THE SEA . . . I LEVEL OUT AT TWENTY FEET ABOVE THE WATER . . . EXCEPT FOR HIGH CIRRUS WISPS, THE SKY IS UNIFORMLY BLUE. INSTRUMENT NEEDLES ALL POINT TO THEIR PROPER MARKS. MY PLANS ARE LAID. NOW, FOR ALMOST TWO HUNDRED MILES, UNTIL NEWFOUNDLAND'S COAST APPEARS, I'LL HAVE NOTHING TO DO BUT FOLLOW THE COMPASS AND ADD ONE SET OF READINGS TO MY LOG . . . SLEEP COMES FILTERING IN . . . IF I COULD THROW MYSELF DOWN ON A BED, I'D BE ASLEEP IN AN INSTANT. IN FACT, IF I DIDN'T KNOW THE RESULT, I'D FALL ASLEEP JUST AS I AM, SITTING UP IN THE COCKPIT — I'M BEYOND THE STAGE WHERE I NEED A BED, OR EVEN TO LIE DOWN. MY EYES FEEL DRY AND HARD AS STONES. THE LIDS PULL DOWN WITH POUNDS OF WEIGHT

AGAINST THEIR MUSCLES. KEEPING THEM OPEN IS LIKE HOLDING ARMS OUTSTRETCHED WITHOUT SUPPORT. AFTER A MINUTE OR TWO OF EFFORT, I HAVE TO LET THEM CLOSE. THEN, I PRESS THEM TIGHTLY TOGETHER, FORCING MY MIND TO THINK ABOUT WHAT I'M DOING SO I WON'T FORGET TO OPEN THEM AGAIN . . . I TRY LETTING ONE EYELID CLOSE AT A TIME WHILE I PROP THE OTHER OPEN WITH MY WILL. BUT THE EFFORT'S TOO MUCH. SLEEP IS WINNING. MY WHOLE BODY ARGUES DULLY THAT NOTHING . . . IS QUITE SO DESIRABLE AS SLEEP. MY MIND IS LOSING RESOLUTION AND CONTROL . . . IF SLEEP WEIGHS SO HEAVILY ON ME NOW, HOW CAN I GET THROUGH THE NIGHT, TO SAY NOTHING OF THE DAWN, AND ANOTHER DAY AND ITS NIGHT, AND POSSIBLY EVEN THE DAY AFTER? SOMETHING MUST BE DONE — IMMEDIATELY . . . I WILL *FORCE* MY BODY TO REMAIN ALERT. I WILL *FORCE* MY MIND TO CONCENTRATE . . . I SIMPLY CAN'T THINK OF SLEEP . . . THE FIRST QUARTER OF MY FLIGHT IS BEHIND . . . IN ANOTHER THREE HOURS, I LEAVE NEWFOUNDLAND BEHIND AND START OVER NEARLY 2,000 MILES OF OCEAN.

THE TENTH HOUR: *Over the Atlantic*

NINE HOURS OF FUEL BURNED. THAT MEANS ABOUT 800 POUNDS LESS LOAD. THE PLANE FEELS LIGHTER . . .

THE TWELFTH HOUR: *Over Newfoundland*

I'VE COVERED 1,100 MILES IN 11 HOURS. THAT'S AN AVERAGE OF EXACTLY 100 MILES AN HOUR IN SPITE OF THE DETOURS I HAD TO MAKE AROUND STORMS IN NOVA SCOTIA.

THE THIRTEENTH HOUR: *Over the Atlantic*

ONE-THIRD OF THE FLIGHT COMPLETE . . . INSTRUMENT READINGS ARE ALL NORMAL. THE ENGINE SOUNDS SMOOTHER THAN AT THE BEGINNING OF THE FLIGHT.

THE FOURTEENTH HOUR: *Over the Atlantic*

IT'S COLD UP HERE AT — I GLANCE AT THE ALTIMETER — 10,500 FEET . . . *COLD* . . . GOOD LORD, THERE *ARE* THINGS TO BE CONSIDERED OUTSIDE THE COCKPIT! HOW COULD I FORGET! I JERK OFF A LEATHER MITTEN AND THRUST MY ARM OUT THE WINDOW. MY PALM IS COVERED WITH STING-ING PIN PRICKS. I PULL THE FLASHLIGHT FROM MY POCKET AND THROW ITS BEAM ONTO A STRUT. THE ENGINE'S EDGE IS IRREGULAR AND SHINY — *ICE!* . . . I'VE GOT TO TURN AROUND, GET BACK INTO THE CLEAR AIR . . . I THROW MY FLASHLIGHT ONTO THE WING STRUT. ICE IS THICKER! . . . FOR THE FIRST TIME, THE THOUGHT OF TURNING BACK SERIOUSLY ENTERS MY MIND. . . . THINK OF FLYING LONG ENOUGH TO REACH IRELAND, AND ENDING UP AT ROOSE-VELT FIELD!

THE SIXTEENTH HOUR: *Over the Atlantic*

FIFTEEN HUNDRED MILES BEHIND. TWO THOUSAND ONE HUNDRED MILES TO GO. I'M HALFWAY TO EUROPE; NOT HALF WAY ACROSS THE OCEAN OR HALFWAY TO PARIS, BUT HALFWAY BETWEEN NEW YORK AND IRELAND . . . I SHAKE MYSELF VIOLENTLY, ASHAMED AT MY WEAKNESS . . . HOW COULD I EVER FACE MY PARTNERS AND SAY THAT I HAD FAILED TO REACH PARIS BECAUSE I WAS SLEEPY? . . . I CUP MY HAND INTO THE SLIPSTREAM, DIVERTING A STRONG

CURRENT OF AIR AGAINST MY FACE, BREATHING DEEPLY OF ITS GUSTY FRESHNESS. I LET MY EYELIDS FALL SHUT FOR FIVE SECONDS; THEN RAISE THEM AGAINST TONS OF WEIGHT. PROTESTING, THEY WON'T OPEN WIDE UNTIL I FORCE THEM WITH MY THUMB, AND LIFT THE MUSCLES OF MY FOREHEAD TO HELP KEEP THEM IN PLACE. SLEEP OVERCOMES MY RESISTANCE LIKE A DRUG. MY FINGERS ARE COLD FROM THE SLIPSTREAM. I DRAW MY MITTENS ON AGAIN. SHALL I PUT ON FLYING BOOTS? BUT I'D HAVE TO UNBUCKLE THE SAFETY BELT AND TAKE MY FEET OFF THE RUBBER PEDALS, AND DO MOST OF THE WORK WITH ONE HAND. THE *SPIRIT OF ST. LOUIS* WOULD VEER OFF COURSE AND I'D HAVE TO STRAIGHTEN IT OUT A DOZEN TIMES BEFORE I GOT THE BOOTS ON. IT'S TOO MUCH EFFORT. I'D RATHER BE A LITTLE COLD.

THE SEVENTEENTH HOUR:
Over the Atlantic

IT'S MIDNIGHT IN NEW YORK . . . HERE, IT'S TWO O'CLOCK IN THE MORNING . . . DAWN ISN'T MANY HOURS AWAY. THE MOONLIGHT IS BRILLIANT. OBJECTS IN MY COCKPIT ARE TAKING FORM AGAIN; I CAN ALMOST READ THE FIGURES ON THE CHARTS. ONLY CORNERS AND OUT OF THE WAY PLACES REMAIN HIDDEN IN THE DARKNESS . . . I THROW MY FLASHLIGHT OUT ONTO THE WING STRUTS. THERE'S NO TRACE OF ICE REMAINING. IT'S WARMER IN THE COCKPIT; PLEASANTLY WARM. MY HANDS ARE WARM TOO, AND MOIST. I PULL OFF MY MITTENS AND PRESS AN ARM OUT AGAINST THE SLIPSTREAM . . . IT HAS MORE THE FEEL OF A TROPICAL SEA. IT'S CHANGED COMPLETELY WITHIN THE HOUR, LIKE THE CLOUDS. IT'S FRIENDLY, RELAXING AIR — NO DANGER OF ICE; NO PIN

PRICKS ON THE PALM. I LAY MY MITTENS ON THE FLOOR AND
ZIP DOWN MY FLYING SUIT.

THE EIGHTEENTH HOUR:
Over the Atlantic

IN ONE MORE HOUR I'LL BE HALFWAY TO PARIS . . . FOR
UNMEASURABLE PERIODS, I SEEM DIVORCED FROM MY BODY,
AS THOUGH I WERE AN AWARENESS SPREADING OUT
THROUGH SPACE, OVER THE EARTH AND INTO THE HEAVENS,
UNHAMPERED BY TIME OR SUBSTANCE, FREE FROM THE
GRAVITATION THAT BINDS MEN TO HEAVY HUMAN PROBLEMS
OF THE WORLD. MY BODY REQUIRES NO ATTENTION . . . THE
UNCONTROLLABLE DESIRE TO SLEEP FALLS OVER ME IN
QUILTED LAYERS. I'VE BEEN STAVING IT OFF WITH DIFFICULTY
DURING THE HOURS OF MOONLIGHT. NOW IT LOOMS ALL
BUT INSURMOUNTABLE. THIS IS THE HOUR I'VE BEEN
DREADING; THE HOUR AGAINST WHICH I'VE TRIED TO STEEL
MYSELF. I KNOW IT'S THE BEGINNING OF MY GREATEST TEST.
THIS WILL BE THE WORST TIME OF ALL, THIS EARLY HOUR OF
THE SECOND MORNING — THE THIRD MORNING, IT IS,
SINCE I'VE SLEPT. I'VE LOST COMMAND OF MY EYELIDS.
WHEN THEY START TO CLOSE, I CAN'T RESTRAIN THEM.
THEY SHUT, AND I SHAKE MYSELF, AND LIFT THEM WITH MY
FINGERS . . . LIDS CLOSE AGAIN REGARDLESS, STICK TIGHT AS
THOUGH WITH GLUE. MY BODY HAS REVOLTED FROM THE
RULE OF ITS MIND — ALL I WANT IN LIFE IS TO THROW MY-
SELF DOWN FLAT, STRETCH OUT — AND SLEEP . . .

I'VE *GOT* TO FIND SOME WAY TO KEEP ALERT. THERE'S NO
ALTERNATIVE BUT DEATH AND FAILURE. *NO ALTERNATIVE
BUT DEATH AND FAILURE,* I KEEP REPEATING, USING THE

THOUGHT AS A WHIP ON MY LAGGING MIND; TRYING TO MAKE MY SENSES REALIZE THE IMPORTANCE OF WHAT I'M SAYING . . . I TRY RUNNING FAST ON THE FLOOR BOARDS WITH MY FEET FOR AS MANY SECONDS AS THE *SPIRIT OF ST. LOUIS* WILL HOLD TO COURSE. THEN, I CLAMP THE STICK BETWEEN MY KNEES WHILE I SIMULATE RUNNING WITH MY HANDS, I PUSH FIRST ONE WING LOW AND THEN THE OTHER, TO BLOW FRESH AIR THROUGH THE COCKPIT AND CHANGE PRESSURES ON MY BODY. I SHAKE MY HEAD UNTIL IT HURTS, RUB THE MUSCLES OF MY FACE TO REGAIN FEELING. I PULL THE COTTON FROM MY EARS, FLUFF IT OUT, AND WAD IT IN AGAIN.

I TAKE OFF MY HELMET — RUB MY HEAD — PULL THE HELMET ON AGAIN — I DRINK SOME WATER FROM THE CANTEEN — THAT HELPS. POSSIBLY IF I EAT A SANDWICH — THE GREASE SPOTTED BAG LIES UNOPENED AT MY SIDE. I'VE HAD NOTHING SINCE BREAKFAST YESTERDAY; BUT MY MOUTH WANTS NO FOOD, AND EATING MIGHT MAKE ME SLEEPIER. SHOULD I HAVE TAKEN ALONG A THERMOS OF COFFEE? WOULD THAT KEEP ME AWAKE? NO, I DON'T WANT COFFEE EITHER. IT WOULDN'T DO ANY GOOD. IT WOULDN'T HAVE ANY EFFECT WHEN I'M FEELING LIKE THIS. COFFEE MAY BE ALL RIGHT FOR SCHOOL PRE-EXAMINATION NIGHTS; BUT IT WOULD BE WORSE THAN USELESS HERE. SHAKING MY BODY AND STAMPING MY FEET NO LONGER HAS EFFECT. IT'S MORE FATIGUING THAN AROUSING. I'LL HAVE TO TRY SOMETHING ELSE. I PUSH THE STICK FORWARD AND DIVE DOWN INTO A HIGH RIDGE OF CLOUD, PULLING UP SHARPLY AFTER I CLIP THROUGH ITS SUMMIT. THAT WAKES ME A LITTLE, BUT TRICKS DON'T HELP FOR LONG. THEY'RE ONLY TIRING. IT'S BETTER TO SIT STILL AND CONSERVE STRENGTH.

THE NINETEENTH HOUR:
Over the Atlantic

HALFWAY TO PARIS . . . SHALL I SHIFT FUEL TANKS AGAIN? I'VE BEEN RUNNING A LONG TIME ON THE FUSELAGE TANK. I PUT ANOTHER PENCIL MARK ON THE INSTRUMENT BOARD TO REGISTER THE EIGHTEENTH HOUR OF FUEL CON- SUMED . . .

DURING THE GROWTH OF MORNING TWILIGHT, I LOSE THE SENSE OF TIME. THERE ARE PERIODS WHEN IT SEEMS I'M FLYING THROUGH ALL SPACE, THROUGH ALL ETERNITY.

THE TWENTIETH HOUR:
Over the Atlantic

THIS IS MORNING — THE TIME TO DESCEND AND MAKE CONTACT WITH THE OCEAN . . . IT'S A FIERCE, UNFRIENDLY SEA — A SEA THAT WOULD BATTER THE LARGEST OCEAN LINER. I FEEL NAKED ABOVE IT . . . THIS WOULD BE A HELLISH PLACE TO LAND IF THE ENGINE FAILED.

NO! NO, I CAN'T LIE DOWN AND SLEEP! NO! NO, I CAN'T GET OUT AND WALK. RUB YOUR EYES, SHAKE YOUR HEAD. YOU'RE OVER THE MIDDLE OF AN OCEAN!

THE TWENTY-SECOND HOUR:
Over the Atlantic

WHILE I'M STARING AT THE INSTRUMENTS, DURING AN UN- EARTHLY AGE OF TIME, BOTH CONSCIOUS AND ASLEEP, THE FUSELAGE BEHIND ME BECOMES FILLED WITH GHOSTLY PRES- ENCES — VAGUELY OUTLINED FORMS, TRANSPARENT, MOV- ING, RIDING WEIGHTLESS WITH ME IN THE PLANE. I FEEL NO SURPRISE AT THEIR COMING. THERE'S NO SUDDENNESS TO

THEIR APPEARANCE. WITHOUT TURNING MY HEAD, I SEE
THEM AS CLEARLY AS THOUGH IN MY NORMAL FIELD OF VI-
SION. THERE'S NO LIMIT TO MY SIGHT — MY SKULL IS ONE
GREAT EYE, SEEING EVERYWHERE AT ONCE.

THESE PHANTOMS SPEAK WITH HUMAN VOICES — FRIENDLY
VAPOR-LIKE SHAPES, WITHOUT SUBSTANCE, ABLE TO VANISH
OR APPEAR AT WILL, TO PASS IN AND OUT THROUGH THE WALLS
OF THE FUSELAGE AS THOUGH NO WALLS WERE THERE. NOW,
MANY ARE CROWDED BEHIND ME. NOW, ONLY A FEW REMAIN.
FIRST ONE AND THEN ANOTHER PRESSES FORWARD TO MY
SHOULDER TO SPEAK ABOVE THE ENGINE'S NOISE, AND THEN
DRAWS BACK AMONG THE GROUP BEHIND. AT TIMES, VOICES
COME OUT OF THE AIR ITSELF, CLEAR YET FAR AWAY, TRAVEL-
ING THROUGH DISTANCES THAT CAN'T BE MEASURED BY THE
SCALE OF HUMAN MILES; FAMILIAR VOICES, CONVERSING AND
ADVISING ON MY FLIGHT, DISCUSSING PROBLEMS OF MY NAV-
IGATION, REASSURING ME, GIVING ME MESSAGES OF IMPOR-
TANCE UNATTAINABLE IN ORDINARY LIFE . . . APPREHENSION
SPREADS OVER TIME AND SPACE UNTIL THEIR OLD MEANINGS
DISAPPEAR. I'M NOT CONSCIOUS OF TIME'S DIRECTION.

THE TWENTY-FOURTH HOUR:
Over the Atlantic

TWENTY-THREE HUNDRED MILES FROM NEW YORK. THIR-
TEEN HUNDRED MILES TO PARIS.

THE TWENTY-FIFTH HOUR:
Over the Atlantic

I SHIFT BACK TO THE RIGHT-WING TANK, AND MARK AN-
OTHER LINE ON THE INSTRUMENT BOARD. NOW TO FILL IN

THE LOG — NO, NAVIGATION IS MORE IMPORTANT. I'LL LAY
OUT PLANS WHILE MY MIND IS CLEAR.

THE TWENTY-SEVENTH HOUR:
Over the Atlantic

THE GREATEST TEST OF MY NAVIGATION WILL COME IF I
MAKE A LANDFALL IN DARKNESS, WHEN HILLS MERGE INTO
VALLEYS AND RAILROAD INTERSECTIONS ARE IMPOSSIBLE TO
SEE. THEN, I'LL HAVE TO KEEP A SHARP WATCH AHEAD TO
AVOID FLYING INTO SOME HILL OR MOUNTAIN . . .

I'M FLYING ALONG DREAMILY WHEN IT CATCHES MY EYE,
THAT BLACK SPECK ON THE WATER TWO OR THREE MILES
SOUTHEAST . . . SECONDS PASS BEFORE MY MIND TAKES IN
THE FULL IMPORTANCE OF WHAT MY EYES ARE SEEING . . .
FISHING BOATS! *THE COAST, THE EUROPEAN COAST, CAN'T BE
FAR AWAY!* THE OCEAN IS BEHIND, THE FLIGHT COMPLETED.
THOSE LITTLE VESSELS, THOSE CHIPS ON THE SEA, ARE EU-
ROPE. WHAT NATIONALITY? ARE THEY IRISH, ENGLISH,
SCOTCH OR FRENCH? CAN THEY BE FROM NORWAY, OR
FROM SPAIN? THE FIRST BOAT IS LESS THAN A MILE AHEAD —
I CAN SEE ITS MAST AND CABIN. I CAN SEE IT ROCKING ON
THE WATER . . . BUT WHERE IS THE CREW? THERE'S NO SIGN
OF LIFE ON DECK . . .

I FLY OVER TO THE NEXT BOAT BOBBING UP AND DOWN
ON THE SWELLS. ITS DECK IS EMPTY TOO. BUT AS I DROP MY
WING TO CIRCLE, A MAN'S HEAD APPEARS, THRUST OUT
THROUGH A CABIN PORTHOLE, MOTIONLESS, STARING UP AT
ME . . . I GLIDE DOWN WITHIN FIFTY FEET OF THE CABIN,
CLOSE THE THROTTLE AND SHOUT AS LOUDLY AS I CAN:
WHICH WAY IS IRELAND?

THE TWENTY-EIGHTH HOUR:
Over the Atlantic

IS THAT A CLOUD ON THE NORTHEASTERN HORIZON, OR A STRIP OF LOW FOG — OR — *CAN IT POSSIBLY BE LAND?* IT LOOKS LIKE LAND . . . I'VE CLIMBED TO TWO THOUSAND FEET SO I CAN SEE THE CONTOURS OF THE COUNTRY BETTER. THE MOUNTAINS ARE OLD AND ROUNDED; THE FARMS SMALL AND STONY. RAIN-GLISTENED DIRT ROADS WIND NARROWLY THROUGH HILLS AND FIELDS. BELOW ME LIES A GREAT TAPER- ING BAY; A LONG, BOULDERED ISLAND; A VILLAGE. YES, THERE'S A PLACE ON THE CHART WHERE IT ALL FITS.

I CAN HARDLY BELIEVE IT'S TRUE. I'M ALMOST EXACTLY ON MY ROUTE, CLOSER THAN I HAD HOPED TO COME IN MY WILDEST DREAMS BACK IN SAN DIEGO.

THE THIRTIETH HOUR:
Over St. George's Channel

IT'S 12:52 P.M. NEW YORK TIME; ABOUT 5:30 HERE. I'M JUST OVER FOUR HOURS FROM PARIS, BY TURNING THE ENGINE FASTER, I CAN REACH FRANCE BEFORE DARKNESS . . . ALL READINGS ARE NORMAL . . . AT ANY MOMENT NOW ENG- LAND'S SHORE LINE WILL BE IN SIGHT.

THE THIRTY-FIRST HOUR:
Over England

ONE MORE HOUR TO THE COAST OF FRANCE! . . . ONLY THREE HUNDRED MILES TO PARIS. THE HORIZON IS SHARP- ENING, AND THE SKY AHEAD IS CLEAR.

THE THIRTY-SECOND HOUR:
Over the English Channel

A STRIP OF LAND, TEN MILES OR SO IN WIDTH, DENTS THE HORIZON — THE COAST OF *FRANCE!* IT COMES LIKE AN OUT-STRETCHED HAND TO MEET ME, GLOWING IN THE LIGHT OF SUNSET.

THE THIRTY-THIRD HOUR:
Over France

ALMOST THIRTY-FIVE HUNDRED MILES FROM NEW YORK. I'VE BROKEN THE WORLD DISTANCE RECORD FOR A NON-STOP AIRPLANE FLIGHT . . . IN ONE HOUR MORE I SHOULD SEE THE LIGHTS OF PARIS . . .

I NOSE THE *SPIRIT OF ST. LOUIS* LOWER, WHILE I STUDY THE FARMS AND VILLAGES . . . PEOPLE COME RUNNING OUT AS I SKIM LOW OVER THEIR HOUSES — BLUE-JEANED PEAS-ANTS, WHITE-APRONED WIVES, CHILDREN SCRAMBLING BE-TWEEN THEM, ALL BAREHEADED AND LOOKING AS THOUGH THEY'D JUMPED UP FROM THE SUPPER TABLE TO SEARCH FOR THE NOISE ABOVE THEIR ROOFS . . .

I PUSH THE STICK FORWARD, CLAMP IT BETWEEN MY KNEES AGAIN, AND UNCORK THE CANTEEN. I CAN DRINK ALL THE WATER I WANT, NOW — PLENTY MORE BELOW IF I SHOULD BE FORCED DOWN BETWEEN HERE AND PARIS. BUT HOW FLAT THE SANDWICH TASTES! BREAD AND MEAT NEVER TOUCHED MY TONGUE LIKE THIS BEFORE. IT'S AN EFFORT EVEN TO SWALLOW. I'M HUNGRY, BECAUSE I GO ON EATING, BUT I HAVE TO WASH EACH MOUTHFUL DOWN WITH WATER . . . ONE SANDWICH IS ENOUGH. I BRUSH THE CRUMBS OFF MY LAP. I START TO THROW THE WRAPPING THROUGH THE WINDOW — NO, THESE FIELDS ARE SO CLEAN

AND FRESH IT'S A SHAME TO SCATTER THEM WITH PAPER. I CRUNCH IT UP AND STUFF IT BACK IN THE BROWN BAG. I DON'T WANT THE LITTER FROM A SANDWICH TO SYMBOLIZE MY FIRST CONTACT WITH FRANCE.

ALL DETAILS ON THE GROUND ARE MASKING OUT IN NIGHT. COLOR IS GONE. ONLY SHADES REMAIN — WOODS, DARKER THAN FIELDS; HEDGE ROWS, LINES OF BLACK. LIGHTS TWINKLE IN VILLAGES AND BLINK IN FARM HOUSE WINDOWS. MY INSTRUMENTS ARE LUMINOUS AGAIN. THE REST OF THE FLIGHT WILL BE IN DARKNESS. BUT I CAN'T MISS PARIS, EVEN IF I FIND NO OTHER CHECK POINT ON MY ROUTE. I'M TOO CLOSE. THE SKY'S TOO CLEAR. THE CITY IS TOO LARGE.

I'M STILL FLYING AT FOUR THOUSAND FEET WHEN I SEE IT, THAT SCARCELY PERCEPTIBLE GLOW, AS THOUGH THE MOON HAD RUSHED AHEAD OF SCHEDULE. PARIS IS RISING OVER THE EDGE OF THE EARTH . . . GRADUALLY AVENUES, PARKS, AND BUILDINGS TAKE OUTLINE FORM; AND THERE, FAR BELOW, A LITTLE OFFSET FROM THE CENTER, IS A COLUMN OF LIGHTS POINTING UPWARD, CHANGING ANGLES AS I FLY — THE EIFFEL TOWER. I CIRCLE ONCE ABOVE IT, AND TURN NORTHEASTWARD TOWARD LE BOURGET.

THE THIRTY-FOURTH HOUR:
Over France

LE BOURGET ISN'T SHOWN ON MY MAP. NO ONE I TALKED TO BACK HOME HAD MORE THAN A GENERAL IDEA OF ITS LOCATION. IT'S A BIG AIRPORT, I WAS TOLD YOU CAN'T MISS IT. JUST FLY NORTHEAST FROM THE CITY. SO I PENCILED A CIRCLE ON MY MAP, ABOUT WHERE LE BOURGET OUGHT TO BE; AND NOW THE *SPIRIT OF ST. LOUIS* IS OVER THE OUT-

SKIRTS OF PARIS, POINTED TOWARD THE CENTER OF THAT CIRCLE.

I LOOK AHEAD. A BEACON SHOULD BE FLASHING ON SUCH A LARGE AND IMPORTANT AIRPORT. BUT THE NEAREST BEACON I SEE IS FULLY TWENTY MILES AWAY, AND WEST INSTEAD OF EAST OF PARIS . . .

YES, THERE'S A BLACK PATCH TO MY LEFT, LARGE ENOUGH TO BE THE AIRPORT. AND THERE ARE LIGHTS ALL AROUND IT. BUT THEY'RE NEITHER STRAIGHT NOR REGULARLY SPACED, AND SOME ARE STRANGELY CROWDED TOGETHER. BUT IF THAT'S NOT LE BOURGET, WHERE ELSE CAN IT BE? . . . IT LOOKS LIKE AN AIRPORT . . . THIS IS IN THE RIGHT DIRECTION WHERE LE BOURGET OUGHT TO BE; BUT I EXPECTED TO FIND IT FARTHER OUT FROM THE CITY. I'LL FLY ON NORTHEAST A FEW MILES MORE. THEN, IF I SEE NOTHING ELSE THAT LOOKS LIKE AN AIRPORT, I'LL COME BACK AND CIRCLE AT LOWER ALTITUDE.

. . . YES, IT'S DEFINITELY AN AIRPORT. I SEE PART OF A CONCRETE APRON IN FRONT OF A LARGE, HALFOPEN DOOR. BUT IS IT LE BOURGET? WELL, AT LEAST IT'S A PARIS AIRPORT. THAT'S THE IMPORTANT THING. IT'S PARIS I SET OUT FOR. IF I LAND ON THE WRONG FIELD, IT WON'T BE TOO SERIOUS AN ERROR — AS LONG AS I LAND SAFELY. I LOOK AROUND ONCE MORE FOR OTHER FLOODLIGHTS OR A BEACON. THERE ARE NONE — NOTHING EVEN WORTH FLYING OVER TO INVESTIGATE. I SPIRAL LOWER, LEFT WING DOWN, KEEPING CLOSE TO THE EDGE OF THE FIELD. THERE AREN'T LIKELY TO BE ANY RADIO TOWERS NEARBY. I'LL GIVE THOSE LIGHTS ALONG THE SOUTHERN BORDER A WIDE BERTH WHEN I COME IN TO LAND. THERE MAY BE HIGH FACTORY CHIMNEYS RISING AMONG THEM . . . IT *MUST* BE LE BOURGET.

I CIRCLE SEVERAL TIMES WHILE I LOSE ALTITUDE, TRYING TO PENETRATE THE SHADOWS FROM DIFFERENT VANTAGE POINTS, GETTING THE LAY OF THE LAND AS WELL AS I CAN IN DARKNESS. AT ONE THOUSAND FEET I DISCOVER THE WIND SOCK, DIMLY LIGHTED, ON TOP OF SOME BUILDING. IT'S BULGED, BUT FAR FROM STIFF. THAT MEANS A GENTLE, CONSTANT WIND, NOT OVER TEN OR FIFTEEN MILES AN HOUR. MY LANDING DIRECTION WILL BE OVER THE FLOOD-LIGHTS, ANGLING AWAY FROM THE HANGAR LINE. WHY CIR-CLE ANY LONGER? THAT'S ALL THE INFORMATION I NEED. NO MATTER HOW HARD I TRY, MY EYES CAN'T PENETRATE THE BLANKET OF NIGHT OVER THE CENTRAL PORTION OF THE FIELD . . . IT'S ONLY A HUNDRED YARDS TO THE HAN-GARS NOW — SOLID FORMS EMERGING FROM THE NIGHT. I'M TOO HIGH — TOO FAST. DROP WING — LEFT RUD-DER — SIDESLIP — CAREFUL — MUSTN'T GET ANYWHERE NEAR THE STALL. I'VE NEVER LANDED THE *SPIRIT OF ST. LOUIS* AT NIGHT BEFORE . . . CAREFUL — EASY TO BOUNCE WHEN YOU'RE TIRED — STILL TOO FAST — TAIL TOO HIGH — HOLD OFF — HOLD OFF — THE WHEELS TOUCH GENTLY — OFF AGAIN — NO, I'LL KEEP CONTACT — EASE THE STICK FORWARD — BACK ON THE GROUND OFF — BACK . . . NOT A BAD LANDING, BUT I'M BEYOND THE LIGHT — CAN'T SEE ANYTHING AHEAD . . . THE *SPIRIT OF ST. LOUIS* SWINGS AROUND AND STOPS ROLLING, RESTING ON THE SOLIDNESS OF EARTH, IN THE CENTER OF LE BOUR-GET . . .

I START TO TAXI BACK TOWARD THE FLOODLIGHTS AND HANGARS — BUT THE ENTIRE FIELD AHEAD IS COVERED WITH RUNNING FIGURES!

— Charles Lindbergh

Chapter Six

$\mathscr{T}$ H E $\mathscr{H}$ E R O

You are in for it now . . . You're the great American idol.
Your time is no longer your own.
— Richard Blythe, Lindbergh's public relations advisor

I don't know about the idol part . . . But I do know I'm in
a terrible mess.
— Charles Lindbergh

EUROPE

Charles Lindbergh touched down, ahead of schedule, at
10:22 P.M. (Paris time). He thought that some French aviators and, perhaps, a handful of reporters might be on hand
to meet him. He didn't have a visa, so he was a little worried about customs. He had even brought letters of intro-
duction, which he thought might help. He hoped that by

using sign language he would be able to find a hangar for his plane and a hotel for himself.

To his amazement, between 20,000 and 100,000 French men and women had come to Le Bourget Aérodrome to welcome him. Accurate reports of his progress since Ireland had helped swell the size of the crowd. Thousands broke through the barricades and rushed onto the landing field. Thousands more, still in their cars, clogged the roads leading to the airport. He had seen the headlights while circling to land, but hadn't realized they had anything to do with him.

When he climbed out of the cockpit he was taken by the crowd and held aloft. Two French flyers were able to get him released, but only after another American had been

Thousands came to greet Lindbergh when he touched down. They had heard reports of him being last spotted over St. John's, Newfoundland.

The front page of The New York Times *on Sunday, May 22, 1927.*

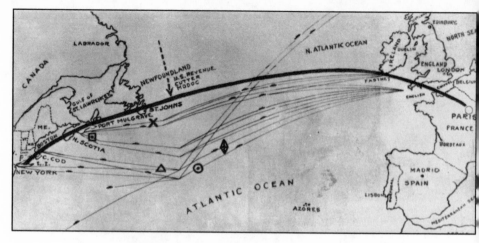

Map of Lindbergh's route. Dark line indicates the Spirit of St. Louis's *course, while thinner lines show regular shipping lanes.*

mistaken for him. Lindbergh's helmet had somehow gotten on the other man's head, and he was being dragged away by the crowd, protesting that he was Henry Wheeler — not Charles Lindbergh. Despite his protests, he was delivered to the waiting American ambassador and eventually released.

In the meantime the real Charles Lindbergh was insisting that something be done about his plane before he agreed to leave the field. He was shocked when he saw the *Spirit of St. Louis.* The crowds had ripped holes in the fuselage in order to take home souvenirs. What angered him even more was that the navigation log he had kept during his flight had been stolen. The French police, responding to Lindbergh's requests, saw to it that no further damage was done to his plane.

The French flyers drove Lindbergh by back roads to the ambassador's residence. It was impossible to use any of the main roads — Lindbergh's landing had created the worst traffic jam in the history of Paris.

Lindbergh slept for the next ten hours. In the morning Lindbergh (wearing a suit someone had lent him) and the ambassador stood on the balcony and greeted the jubilant crowd that had gathered in front of the embassy. He made sure to take the time, that first, tumultuous day, to visit Nungesser's mother and console her as best he could. After Paris he was given rousing receptions in Brussels and London. The King of England, unable or unwilling to contain his curiosity, asked Lindbergh how he had peed; in an aluminum container, was the answer.

> Even the eight days . . . in New York, had not prepared me for the worldwide interest and tremendous publicity my successful landing in Paris caused. I had planned to spend the night in some hotel. Instead, I slept in the American Embassy . . . I thought most of my days in France would be passed on flying fields

U.S. Ambassador Myron T. Herrick leads a congratulatory cheer for Lindbergh (wearing his borrowed suit) in front of the American Embassy in Paris.

with French pilots. Instead, I received such an extraordinary welcome that its lunches, dinners, and ceremonies left hardly any time to be with my plane.

— Charles Lindbergh

AMERICA

Lindbergh had planned to fly back to the United States via Europe, Siberia, Alaska, and Canada, thus completing a trip around the world. However, he reluctantly gave in to pressure from the ambassador to accept President Calvin Coolidge's invitation to return aboard the cruiser USS *Memphis.*

The now world-famous Lindbergh drew crowds like this one that surrounded his plane at Croyden Airdrome in London, England, May 29, 1927.

48 HOME COMERS!
One for every State

President Coolidge pins on the Distinguished Flying Cross at the awards ceremony in Washington, D.C.

And so, on June 4, 1927, with the *Spirit of St. Louis* packed in a wooden crate and strapped to the deck, the USS *Memphis* left France for the United States, carrying the most famous man in the world.

In Washington, D.C., he was joined by his mother, and the two of them were the personal guests of the president. Enormous and enthusiastic crowds hailed Lindbergh as he rode in an open car down Pennsylvania Avenue, heading for the Washington Monument. He grinned and waved at times, but mostly he looked uncomfortable. The turnout at the monument was the largest in the history of the city. In addition an estimated thirty million listened to the ceremonies over fifty radio stations nationwide.

The president presented him with the Distinguished Flying Cross and the Congressional Medal of Honor (the first time it was awarded for a non-military act), and the Post Office issued an airmail stamp in his honor (the first for a living American).

In New York Harbor he was welcomed by a flotilla of boats: yachts, motorboats, tugs, and fireboats, which shot streams of water in the air. They, along with the city's factories, blew their whistles and horns, making a terrific welcoming din.

Four and a half million people turned out to greet the young hero as he rode up Broadway (still the largest parade in New York's history). Eighteen hundred tons of ticker tape fell from the buildings that lined the parade route. So

New York City's tickertape parade for Lindbergh was the largest ever recorded.

Lindbergh rides up Broadway during the parade in his honor.

many New Yorkers came out to welcome Lindbergh that police feared a rash of burglaries as thieves took advantage of the many empty apartments and houses.

Lindbergh's speeches in Europe, and now in America, were surprisingly short and to the point.

> . . . 132 years ago Benjamin Franklin was asked: "What good is your balloon? What will it accomplish?" He replied: "What good is a newborn child?" Less than twenty years ago when I was not far advanced from infancy M. Blériot flew across the English Channel and was asked: "What good is your aeroplane? What will it accomplish?" Today those same skeptics might ask me what good has been my flight from New York to Paris. My answer is that I believe it is the forerunner of a great air service from America to France, America to Europe, to bring our peoples nearer together in understanding and in friendship than they have ever been.
>
> — Charles Lindbergh

He never spoke of himself, preferring to emphasize the achievements of those who came before and the pivotal role that advancements in American engineering had played in his successful flight. He talked about the topics that concerned him: the international goodwill that he hoped his flight would encourage, the future of aviation in both the United States and Europe, and the construction of passenger airports near major American cities.

He received millions of letters (including marriage proposals — four times as many women as men wrote to Lindbergh) and hundreds of thousands of telegrams. Babies,

How Everygirl would like to have her engagement broken.

Cartoons like this one revealed the public's feelings about the young hero.

parks, streets, schools, and, in at least one case, a mountain peak (in Colorado) and a sandwich (in New York) were named after him. The lindy became the name of the latest dance craze.

He was offered hundreds of thousands of dollars to record the story of the flight (with "The Star-Spangled Banner" played at the beginning and the French national anthem at the end). And he was besieged by cosmetic and cigarette companies, clothing manufacturers, and makers of hats, gloves, shaving cream, and hair oil, all clamoring for him to endorse their products.

Lindbergh turned them all down. He believed that lending his name to advertise products that had nothing to do with his profession might reflect poorly on his integrity:

I was offered fifty thousand dollars to endorse publicly a cigarette, half a million dollars plus ten percent of gross to star in a motion picture. Lecture bureaus would guarantee me an income for a single lecture of many times what I could make annually as a mail pilot. I was advised that if I would enter a political career, there was a good chance I could eventually become president.

What really meant most to me — the development of aviation, or the millions I could make? When I considered the question carefully, I realized that money would always be minor to the other terms of the life I led. I decided to continue concentrating on the development of aviation.

— Charles Lindbergh

He did, however, endorse products that were genuinely associated with his flight: Wright engines, Goodrich tires, AC spark plugs, Mobil Oil, and his pen:

I was able to carry very few things in my *Spirit of St. Louis* but I took special care not to forget my faithful Waterman which was most precious to mark the route on my maps.

— Charles Lindbergh

He earned an estimated $500,000 for his historic flight.

His bravery, youth, modesty, and integrity, in combination with his boyish good looks, impressed the American people, who elevated him to the status of a true national hero. He was *Time* magazine's first Man of the Year.

Lindbergh was uncomfortable with the attention and disliked what he considered silly behavior: women running to get corncobs he had discarded, vandals who damaged his childhood home, and souvenir hunters who took his shirts when he sent them to the laundry. Once there was nearly a riot when word got out where his mother was having her hair done.

He continued to answer questions about flying, but none about his personal life.

He wasn't going to let his new worldwide fame affect him.

Chapter Seven

*A*MBASSADOR OF THE *A*IR

I was just a kid at the time.

— Charles Lindbergh

AIR LINDBERGH

In late July 1927, Charles Lindbergh, anxious to be flying again, began a boldly conceived tour, flying the *Spirit of St. Louis* across the United States. The idea was developed by Lindbergh and millionaire Harry Guggenheim, president of the Daniel Guggenheim Fund for the Promotion of Aeronautics. The Guggenheim Fund would provide most of the financial support for the tour. Guggenheim, a former Navy pilot, now an aviation advocate, had taken an interest in Lindbergh. He also offered Lindbergh the use of his huge Long Island estate. There, in just three weeks, working nearly fifteen-hour days, Lindbergh wrote *We,* his first account of the historic flight. It sold 190,000 copies in two months and eventually earned him $200,000.

Just four days after completing *We,* Lindbergh left on the tour.

The Guggenheim Fund had been established to promote the idea that air travel, like travel by car or train, could be incorporated into daily life. The tour, Lindbergh and Guggenheim believed, would show that flying was now reliable and safe. To dramatically demonstrate this fact, Lindbergh would be spending at least one night in each of the (then) forty-eight states. He pledged to arrive precisely on time at each of the scheduled overnight stops, no matter what the weather conditions.

The three-month tour was carefully planned and the rules spelled out.

Guggenheim sent letters to the mayors of all the cities on the schedule.

"I hope you will pardon me for being so explicit . . . but . . . Colonel Lindbergh is making a very difficult trip . . . with a view to promoting interest in aviation rather than with a view to receiving personal plaudits [which he can best accomplish] by limiting his activities."

Lindbergh would not accept personal invitations for any commercial reasons. In fact, there would be no admission charge for seeing him or his plane. Children and teenagers were given special treatment. They were the future flying generations that Lindbergh and Guggenheim wanted most to reach.

Lindbergh had two concerns — punctuality and safety. He raised these issues at a meeting with Guggenheim and representatives of the U.S. Department of Commerce, which was co-sponsoring the tour:

> We must remember two things. First, we must always be on time — if we have to get up in the middle of the night to do it. We want to show people that aviation can come through on time . . . Now, the second is about landing at airports. Sometimes the crowds forget and rush out on to the field . . . I've seen a propeller kill a man, and I don't intend to have anyone hit by my ship if I can help it. I'd rather skip a city entirely than take a chance by landing into a crowd.
>
> —Charles Lindbergh

Lindbergh made sure the police were thanked for providing the security at the various stops. He also personally saw to it that the flowers and candy that were sent to welcome

A proud group of Americans spells out Lindy in the bleachers as he makes his way to San Diego, September 21, 1927.

him found their way to children in the hospital and other deserving groups.

Lindbergh was paid $50,000 (and would become a consultant for the Guggenheim Fund).

By late October, when the tour ended, he had covered 22,340 miles in 260 hours of flying. Only once, due to fog, had he failed to make good on his promise to arrive on time.

Lindbergh was tireless and unselfish in his efforts to promote the future of civilian aviation. He gave 147 speeches, was honored at 69 dinners, and traveled 1,285 miles in parades, greeting the enormous crowds that turned out wherever he went.

Interest in aviation — already dramatically increased by his flight to Paris — was further heightened by Lindbergh's successful nationwide tour. The use of airmail deliveries increased and, perhaps more importantly, airport construction rose significantly. Conservative estimates are that Lindbergh's tour resulted in over $100,000,000 in new construction. And banks, once reluctant to invest in aviation, were now eager to divert funds in that direction.

An estimated 30,000,000 people came to see Lindbergh and the *Spirit of St. Louis.* Young people, fascinated by their new hero, were introduced to the idea that flying would become a part of their lives as Lindbergh predicted in 1927: "The year will surely come when passengers and mail will fly every day from America to Europe."

MEXICO

Two months later Lindbergh took off from Washington, D.C., for a nonstop flight to Mexico City.

Mexican workers show their appreciation of Mexican President Calles, Ambassador Morrow, and Lindbergh with a sign that reads, "Cementing peace and brotherhood between two sister races."

The trip was suggested by Dwight Morrow, the American ambassador to Mexico. Morrow was concerned about the bad will that characterized U.S.-Mexican relations. He believed a visit by America's world-famous aviator would help mend some fences.

The Mexico flight served a dual purpose for Lindbergh. As America's unofficial ambassador of the air, he was happy to oblige Morrow. He was also interested in the December flight because he wanted to test flying over certain kinds of terrain, along particular routes in winter weather conditions.

The 2,100-mile flight lasted twenty-seven and a half hours. It was an exhausting and hazardous flight. For more than half the time, Lindbergh flew in rain, fog, and darkness. At one point he wandered far off course. A crowd of 150,000 had turned out for Lindbergh's scheduled noon arrival. The invariably on-time Lindbergh had not been spotted.

By 2:00 P.M. Ambassador Morrow was visibly upset, and with good reason. Since Lindbergh's New York to Paris

flight there had been a great deal of sentiment that Lindbergh, now a national treasure, should not do anything as
dangerous as flying. Of course, this was exactly the percep-
tion that Lindbergh wanted to overcome. He had no intention of being grounded. But if something happened on his
flight to Mexico City, Morrow would be blamed.

At last, at 2:40 P.M., Lindbergh touched down in Mexico
City.

ANNE MORROW

I had always taken for granted that someday I would
marry and have a family of my own, but I had not
thought much about it. In fact, I had never been
enough interested in any girl to ask her to go on a date.
At college I was inexperienced and shy, and I was having enough trouble in my studies without taking on
the additional problem of women — you had to learn
to dance, to talk their language, to escort them properly to restaurants and theaters. I preferred to ride my
motorcycle. It was also a lot cheaper.

— Charles Lindbergh

Twenty-five-year-old Charles Lindbergh was looking for
a wife. He approached the subject of marriage as he did
everything else: coolly and scientifically. He had no intention of falling in love with the first girl who came along. He
would wait, watch, and choose carefully. During his forty-
eight-state tour he gave the question of marriage a good
deal of thought. He purposely accepted social invitations,
when possible from families with daughters. He believed

the more choices he had, the better his choice would turn out to be.

Charles was concerned about his prospective bride's family, her health, her hearing, and whether or not she was properly built. In many ways it wasn't much different from choosing an airplane. And, he wanted someone who would learn to fly.

Anne Morrow, Ambassador Morrow's middle daughter, was twenty-one when she met Charles Lindbergh.

I saw standing against the great stone pillar . . . a tall, slim boy in evening dress — so much slimmer, so much taller, so much more poised than I expected. A very refined face, not at all like those grinning "Lindy" pictures — a firm mouth, clear, straight blue eyes, fair

Anne Morrow.

hair, and nice color. Then I went down the line, very
confused and overwhelmed by it all. He did not
smile — just bowed and shook hands.

— Anne Morrow Lindbergh

She was attending Smith College in Northampton,
Massachusetts. The two met briefly at the Morrows' New
York apartment. For a while, the press was reporting a blos-
soming romance between Charles and Elisabeth, Anne's
beautiful older sister.

The second daughter, Anne, was blue-eyed, dark-
haired, extremely pretty, but she stood very much in
the background, as though resting in a shadow thrown
by the sparkling vivacity of her older sister, Elisabeth. . . . I had noticed her casually. She looked so very
young, more of high school than of college age, and
she had not made a deep impression on my conscious
mind. Rationally, I was surprised when I found her
becoming conspicuous in my memory months after I
had left the hospitality of her father's embassy in Mexico. But in the fall of 1928 I began laying plans to meet
her again. She was then staying at her family home at
Englewood, New Jersey.

— Charles Lindbergh

Later Charles and Anne saw each other at the Morrows'
fifty-acre estate in Englewood. He took her flying (they
took off from the Guggenheims' private field where Lindbergh kept his own plane) and for drives in the countryside
near her family's home.

My visit as a guest of the family in Mexico made it proper to telephone directly to the Morrow home. Daughter Anne agreed to go with me on a flight over Long Island the following week.

Achieving my objective with the girl left me confronted with my now ever-present problem of the press. If I were seen with one of Ambassador Morrow's daughters at a New York airport, there would be a terrible hullabaloo about it. A dozen or two reporters and photographers would be rushed out to wait for us to land, and thereafter more silly stories would be published.

For the occasion, I rented a small, open-cockpit plane with a quick take-off and a low landing speed. A friend of a friend of mine on Long Island offered me the use of a horse pasture on his estate. I had to fly under high-tension electric cables after take-off, because of the shortness of the pasture, but once past them we climbed up easily over horse jumps and mansions until we could see both shorelines of Long Island . . .

Our "ground date" a few days later involved an afternoon and evening drive over roads of New Jersey in my air-cooled engine Franklin sedan. When it was over we were engaged to be married.

— Charles Lindbergh

The engagement was announced three months later by Ambassador and Mrs. Morrow.

Anne thought about her upcoming marriage and the man she had chosen to wed:

Apparently I am going to marry Charles Lindbergh. It must seem hysterically funny to you as it did to me, when I consider my opinions on marriage. "A safe marriage," "things in common," "liking the same things," "a quiet life," etc., etc. All those things which I am apparently going against. But they seem to have lost their meaning, or have other definitions. Isn't it funny — why does one marry, anyway? I didn't expect or want anything like this. I think probably that was the trouble. It must be fatal to decide on the kind of man you don't want to marry and the kind of life you don't want to lead. You determinedly turn your back on it, set out in the opposite direction — and come bang up against it, in true Alice in the Looking Glass fashion. And there he is — darn it all — the great Western strong-man-open-spaces type and a life of relentless action! But after all, what am I going to do about it? After all, there he is and I've got to go. I wish I could hurry up and get it over with soon. This horrible, fantastic, absurd publicity and thousands of people telling me how lucky and happy I am.

— Anne Morrow Lindbergh

On May 27, 1929, Ambassador and Mrs. Morrow quietly and informally invited family and close friends over for lunch. Only those who *had* to know were aware that a wedding was about to take place: the pastor who was to perform the ceremony and the dressmaker who made Anne's wedding dress. Evangeline was there as the Morrows' houseguest that weekend.

The ceremony was brief and spare. Afterward, Anne

crouched down on the floor of a borrowed car, so she and Charles could elude the reporters and photographers camped outside the Morrow estate. Lindbergh knew that newsmen were also assigned to watch a plane he had at Roosevelt Field. As a decoy, the day before the wedding, he instructed that it be readied for a flight.

I felt quite sure the press expected me to take my bride on a honeymoon by airplane. Therefore I kept well away from flying fields and airplanes, and decided that a boat would be a good place to spend the first week or two after our wedding. I placed an order secretly . . . through an officer of the Elco Company, for a thirty-six-foot motor cruiser. Aside from two or three top officers of the company, no one was to know who the boat was for.

Newspapers had offered to pay workers at the airport where I kept my plane for any information relating to my activities. Here I saw an opportunity to divide the forces of the press. A day or two before our wedding was to take place, I ordered my Falcon flown to Rochester and left, fully serviced, in a hangar on the airport. As I expected, a number of reporters and photographers followed it. That alerted the press, and rumors spread to the effect that our marriage was imminent. But here the fantasies of reporters played into our hands. They had written so many stories about plans for a highly elaborate wedding that they began to believe their own concoctions. When a few dozen guests arrived at [the Morrow estate] in response to invitations to an afternoon reception, reporters at the gate paid only casual attention. The Morrows were noted for having many friends and for giving parties.

All went according to plan. Anne Morrow and I were married on May 27, 1929, in front of the fireplace in the big parlor . . . Before any of the guests left, we slipped out of the house into the back of a big car and out of the gate without being recognized by reporters standing guard there. I had arranged to have our boat, fully equipped and fueled and provisioned, left at anchor at an isolated spot off the Long Island Sound coast.

— Charles Lindbergh

To be deeply in love is, of course, a great liberating force and the most common experience that frees — or seems to free — young people. The loved one is the liberator. Ideally, both members of a couple in love free each other to new and different worlds. I was no exception to the general rule. The sheer fact of finding myself loved was unbelievable and changed my world, my feelings about life and myself. I was given confidence, strength and almost a new character. The man I was to marry believed in me and what I could do, and consequently I found I could do more than I realized, even in that mysterious outer world that fascinated me but seemed unattainable. He opened the door to real life and although it frightened me, it also beckoned. I had to go.

— Anne Morrow Lindbergh

For ten days Charles and Anne managed to enjoy some privacy, cruising in their new motorboat. But on June 6, a press plane buzzed them while reporters leaned out of the windows. Anne ran down into the cabin while Charles defiantly stayed out on deck. A motorboat hounded them, circling and making waves, for eight hours. They offered to stop if Anne and Charles would pose for one photograph. The honeymoon was over.

THE MEDIA

Relations between Charles Lindbergh and the media, never smooth, had worsened during his national tour and flight to Mexico. Now that relationship had deteriorated even further. Lindbergh had come to loathe the media and the life they had forced him to live.

He and Anne couldn't go to restaurants, movies, plays, or even out for a walk. If they did go out they had to take elaborate precautions. They used false names when staying in hotels (invariably their pillowcases were stolen by souvenir hunters) and used disguises when in the streets. Charles wore hats and eyeglasses with no lenses, slicked his hair with oil, and applied burnt cork to darken his eyebrows. Anne used a scarf and lots of makeup.

He still received a million letters a year, and women still ran after him and screamed "There's Lindy!" whenever they spotted him. He and Anne were followed wherever they went. They feared that their phone was tapped and that servants (the Morrows employed twenty-nine) had been bribed by reporters. At least one reporter had tried to get a

Charles and Anne Morrow Lindbergh were forced to disguise themselves in public in order to avoid the relentless press.

job posing as a prospective servant. It was so bad that a man in California formed the "Let Lindy Alone Club."

When Anne became pregnant, newspapers printed rumors of it, angering Lindbergh even further. Anne gave birth to Charles Augustus Lindbergh, Jr., on June 22, 1930 (Anne's twenty-fourth birthday). Charles, Jr., was born in the Morrows' New York apartment because Anne did not believe that she could have any privacy in a hospital.

The Lindberghs did not publicly acknowledge Charles, Jr.'s, birth.

The baby's name was not released for two weeks. Lindbergh had taken photographs of Charles, Jr., which he developed himself. He handed them out to selected members of the press. Representatives from newspapers that Lindbergh felt had treated him and his wife unfairly were excluded.

Some reporters sympathetic to the Lindberghs advised them to simply give a couple of interviews. These reporters believed that by avoiding the press completely the Lindberghs were making things worse for themselves. Lindbergh refused to take their advice.

Anne concerned herself with the baby's health and welfare. She read books about the proper way to bring up a child and worried about pampering him. She talked and sang to him ("You Must Have Been a Beautiful Baby" — one of the popular songs of the day), which he seemed to enjoy. She noted, happily, that he was a responsive and curious child, who already was beginning to look like Charles.

> When I first saw it I thought, Oh dear it's going to look like me — dark hair and a nose all over its face. But then I discovered what I think is Charles' mouth, and the unmistakable cleft in the chin! So I went to sleep quite happy.
>
> — Anne Morrow Lindbergh

It was, indeed, a happy time.

> And I have been happy — very, very happy all the time since the baby has been born.
>
> — Anne Morrow Lindbergh

AROUND THE WORLD

Lindbergh became a technical advisor for Transcontinental Air Transport, which became known as "The Lindbergh Line" and Pan American Airways, Inc. He surveyed and chose new air routes, helped decide which planes to purchase and where to locate terminals, and was instrumental in establishing the first transcontinental airline service.

At the end of July 1931, Charles and Anne set off on a journey over the Arctic to the Far East, flying a Lockheed Sirius that Lindbergh had specially built. The ambitious trip would take several months. The Lindberghs were surveying a route for possible U.S.-China air travel. Charles, Jr., stayed with the Morrows while his parents were away — Anne was uncomfortable leaving Charlie (as she liked to call him) with his only recently hired nurse, Betty Gow. Anne asked her mother to take a picture once a month and looked forward to receiving letters from her mother reporting on the baby's progress:

> Will you keep some kind of record of his actions . . . ?
> Don't let Betty give him too many toys at once, just one or two, and change them about and don't let people fuss over him or pay attention to his little falls or mistakes, will you? I'm sure you will do it all just right — I'm not worrying.
> — Anne Morrow Lindbergh

> What you say about the baby sounds fine, so well and gay. I like everything you tell me about his playing, exploring your room while you write at your desk. I love to think of that, and crawling over the lawn with his blocks. And describing his curls coming out from his blue cap. All just what I want to hear. I love your dancing him at night. Oh, Mother, don't worry — I am very happy thinking about him with you. I know you will do just what is right for him.
> — Anne Morrow Lindbergh

The Lindberghs just before take-off to the Far East.

Anne left Charlie with her mother also because she believed that he would be shielded from the media by her and by being in their summer home in far-off Maine.

Charles and Anne flew the twin-cockpit Lockheed monoplane, which was equipped with a 600-horsepower engine (almost three times the power of the *Spirit of St. Louis*) and had a maximum speed of 185 miles per hour, a range of 2,000 miles, and pontoons for landing on water. (Most of the flight was over wilderness, where it was safer to land on water.) The pontoons served a double function: They also housed most of the fuel. The Lindberghs wore electrically heated flying suits to protect them from the Arctic cold, and Anne studied nutrition before choosing the food they would bring. She was the copilot, navigator, and radio operator.

Their extensive route took them to Canada, Alaska, Russia, Japan, and China. They flew, at times, in total darkness and through dense fog. They were forced down three times. At scheduled stops they met with aviators, explorers, government officials, and local people — most of whom had never seen a plane before. In China they helped flood victims by flying doctors and medical supplies to the devastated areas.

Three months into the grueling trip Anne received a telegram that her father had suddenly died. The Lindberghs cancelled the rest of the journey and immediately headed back to the United States.

Despite her grief over her father's death, Anne was happy to see her "fat lamb" (her new nickname for her son) when she returned. He had, of course, grown quite a bit, was cutting a tooth, drinking milk from a cup, and beginning to form words.

The baby is beautiful and big: pulls himself up in his crib and in his pen, smiles and plays with people a lot more, waves good-bye when you wave. His hair is curly and golden and his skin tanned and flushed. . . . He distinguishes people much more — will not go to strangers but keeps a firm sweet hold on me or Betty.

—Anne Morrow Lindbergh

It is good to be home — and oh, the baby! He is a boy, a strong independent boy swaggering around on his firm little legs. He did not know us but was not afraid of us — not at all afraid of [Charles], which pleased [Charles] tremendously. He began to take such interest in the baby — playing with him, spoiling him by giving him cornflakes and toast and sugar and jam off his

Charles Lindbergh, Jr., at his first birthday party.

plate in the morning and tossing him up in the air.
After he'd done that once or twice the boy came toward
him with outstretched arms. Den! (Again!) [Charles]
admits the boy is good-looking and pretty interesting.

— Anne Morrow Lindbergh

C. Jr. talks a great deal more . . . I take care of him
more . . . so that he'll know me better. It is such a joy
to hear him calling for "Mummy" instead of "Betty."
And she understands just how I feel about it and helps
me. He says a very firm "uh huh" (for yes) which
sounds quite tough and apparently he gets from me
and a very firm complacent "naw" when he doesn't
want to do something . . . C. Jr. and Sr. have a wonderful time together. . . .

They had a pillow fight the other day, at least
Charles threw pillows at the boy and knocked him
down but he only laughed (which surprised Charles
very much and he was quite proud of him) and picked
up a pillow clumsily and tried to throw it at his father.

— Anne Morrow Lindbergh

And she shared the child's pain when he entered the far
larger universe of school:

The first day he went the children all made a great fuss
of him, crowding around, and the littlest boy who
hitherto had had a fuss made of him punched him in
the back. Charlie sat down and cried. He was utterly
bewildered; that anyone should hurt him *purposely* —
that hadn't entered his life before.

— Anne Morrow Lindbergh

Charles, upon their return, became involved in non-flying pursuits. Elisabeth, Anne's older sister, had a heart attack that caused permanent damage to one of her valves. There was no chance of heart surgery in those days because the technology that would keep the patient's heart pumping during the operation hadn't been invented. Charles, interested in science since his days with Grandfather Land, believed there must be a way something could be done. He learned that Dr. Alexis Carrel, a Nobel-prize-winning French surgeon and scientist, also believed that heart surgery was possible.

Carrel was impressed with Lindbergh's ideas for developing a heart pump that would permit the surgery to be performed. He allowed Lindbergh to use his lab and work with him.

Lindbergh also sought out Robert Goddard. Goddard believed that rockets could be made to travel over long distances — in fact, to reach the moon. Such ideas were considered pure science fiction at that time.

Lindbergh, however, was convinced that Goddard's pioneering experiments were worthy of support. When Lindbergh called him, Goddard thought someone was pulling his leg. His wife didn't believe it when he told her. Lindbergh convinced Harry Guggenheim's father, Daniel, to personally provide Goddard with the money he needed to continue his work.

The Lindberghs also spent time looking for a place to build their first home. Surveying the New Jersey countryside by air, they chose a 400-acre tract in an isolated, heavily wooded area near the small village of Hopewell (pop. 900). Its rural seclusion coupled with its proximity to New

York (under two hours by car and twenty minutes by air —
once Charles built the airfield he planned) made it an ideal
choice.

THE EAGLE'S NEST

The Lindberghs lived in a rented house nearby while their
home was being built.

Most of the week they spent living at the Morrows' Englewood, New Jersey, estate. The ten-room whitewashed
fieldstone house (with a separate wing for the servants) was
nearly complete by February 1932, and they began to spend
weekends there.

So did the press and the public. One paper called it "the
Eagle's Nest," and souvenir hunters stole pieces of the construction material that was lying all around.

One night a Peeping Tom was spotted in one of the windows.

PART TWO: DESCENT

Fame is a kind of death.
— Anne Morrow Lindbergh

Chapter Eight

THE CRIME OF THE CENTURY

THE CRIME

MARCH 1, 1932

The last weekend in February 1932, Charlie caught a cold.
The Lindberghs decided to stay in Hopewell, rather than
return, as usual, to Englewood. Monday night, Anne called
Englewood and asked the baby's nurse to come help her
look after him.

On Tuesday evening, March 1, 1932, Anne and Betty Gow
prepared Charlie for bed at his usual time. Betty rubbed his
chest with medication, put the guards on his thumbs (to
stop him from sucking them), dressed him in the flannel

sleeping suit she had made for him, and pinned his blanket to the mattress so it wouldn't come off in the night.

At 7:30 Betty and I were putting the baby to bed. We closed and bolted all the shutters except on one window where the shutters are warped and won't close. Then I left and went downstairs and sat at the desk in the living room. Betty continued to clean the bathroom etc. until some time between 7:45 and 8:00, when she went in to the baby again to see he was covered. He was fast asleep and covered. Then she went downstairs to supper.

[Charles] was late in coming home, not till 8:20. Then we went upstairs. He washed his hands in the bathroom next to the baby's — we heard nothing — perhaps because of the water. Then downstairs to supper at about 8:35 to 9:10 (at this time Betty was still eating her supper — we were all in the west wing of the house). At 9:10 [Charles] and I went upstairs. [Charles] ran a bath, then went down again. I ran a bath. No noise heard. From about 9:30 to 10 [Charles] was in his study, right next to the window under the baby's; no ladder could have been put up then. Betty . . . [was] upstairs still in the west wing.

At ten Betty went in to the baby, shut the window first, then lit the electric stove, then turned to the bed. It was empty and the sides still up. No blankets taken. She thought [Charles] had taken him for a joke. I did, until I saw his face.

— Anne Morrow Lindbergh

Someone had taken the Lindberghs' baby.

THE CRIME SCENE

I had been sitting in the parlor with my wife. Outside, the wind blew and the night was black. Our house was long, with two stories, enclosed by walls of whitewashed stone and a gray slate roof. We had placed the house on the high edge of an old field within our four hundred acres of abandoned farm and wild woodland.

I went upstairs to the child's nursery, opened the door, and immediately noticed a lifted window. A strange-looking envelope lay on the sill. I looked at the crib. It was empty. I ran downstairs, grabbed my rifle, and went out into the night, first to the nursery end of the house. Under the lifted window I saw a ladder, and saw that it was broken. Obviously, it had collapsed as the kidnapper descended. It looked as though it had been made out of new crating boards.

I realized there was no use going into the woods or trying to follow along roads. The night was too dark and stormy to see or hear anything. I returned to the house and put in an emergency call to the State police.

— Charles Lindbergh

Charles had heard a noise earlier, but had not thought enough of it to see what it was. Anne had heard nothing.

The police found footprints leading away from the house, the ladder, and a chisel which, it was assumed, had been used to pry open the shutter. The footprints had a pattern, as if someone had put a sock or a burlap bag over his or her shoes to avoid leaving any traceable clues.

The ladder had been built in three separate seven-foot

The scene of the crime.

sections that fitted together with dowels so it could be dismantled and carried. Each section was narrower than the one below. It was a clever idea, but poorly and oddly constructed. The craftmanship was shoddy and the slats of wood that were its rungs were eighteen and nineteen inches apart rather than the usual twelve inches. It would be awkward for anyone but a very tall person to use the ladder.

The top slat of the bottom section had split — presumably because of the added weight of the child being taken. The breaking wood, it was assumed, was the noise Lindbergh had said he'd heard.

When the ladder was placed against the wall of the house under the nursery window, it fit into two impressions left in the wet earth.

Detective Joseph Bornmann of the New Jersey State police pictured here with the three parts of the kidnap ladder.

Lindbergh had told Anne and Betty not to touch the envelope on the windowsill, or anything the kidnappers might have touched, hoping the police would be able to find fingerprints. There were none. There was, however, a ransom note in the envelope:

Dear Sir!
Have 50,000 $ redy 25000 $ in 20 $ bills 15000 $ in 10 $ bills and 10000 $ in 5 $ bills. After 2–4 days we will inform you were to deliver the Mony.
We warn you for making anyding public or for notify the Polise the child is in gut care.
Indication for all letters are singnature and 3 holds.

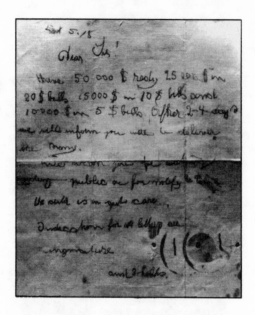

The original ransom note.

By 10:30 P.M., radio programs were being interrupted by news bulletins reporting the kidnapping, and by morning it was front page news being read by a shocked nation. (In the coming weeks newspaper sales would rise as much as twenty percent in some cities and sales of radios would increase dramatically.)

The police awakened the Lindberghs' neighbors and asked if they had seen anything suspicious. State troopers set up roadblocks in New Jersey and New York. All vehicles entering New York City were searched, the drivers questioned, and their license numbers recorded. Hospitals in the area were asked to report if any child fitting the description of the Lindbergh baby was admitted.

A nationwide manhunt for the kidnapper(s) of the Lindbergh baby was underway. As Charles, Jr.'s, description was transmitted via the newspapers, radios, and police teletype, he was spotted in hundreds of locations, some as far away as Michigan, California, and Mexico. Parents with a child his age were stopped and questioned — sometimes repeatedly.

One couple was detained so often the police gave them a note. Another couple who was stopped because their child was thought to resemble the Lindbergh baby made up signs after they were released that said: "See the baby that looks like the Lindbergh baby 15¢." Across the country, drivers were detained simply because their cars had New Jersey license plates.

Meanwhile, back at the Lindbergh home, members of the media flooded the area, joining the growing number of state police and the merely curious, to create a scene of growing confusion. By morning the grounds around the estate were filled with newspaper reporters, photographers, newsreel cameramen, and radio commentators. One news service's entire staff had been assigned to the kidnapping.

Reporters rushed to Hopewell to cover the kidnapping.

Another news service sent ten reporters to cover the case. They rented two ambulances and converted them into mobile photographic darkrooms. Photographs were developed right there, and then, with sirens blaring, rushed to New York. Other news services had motorcycles and chartered planes waiting. The previously quiet village of Hopewell was completely overrun by the media, who rented every available house and apartment.

THE DEPRESSION

The kidnapping took place at the height of the worst economic depression in American history. Between 1930 and 1933, nine thousand banks had been forced to close. Many people lost their life savings. It was a time of widespread unemployment — nearly 13,000,000 were out of work — over twenty-five percent of the workforce. The unemployed, desperate, sold apples on city streets. Seventeen thousand people shined shoes for a living in New York City. The economy grew worse almost every month.

Kidnappings — especially of the wealthy — were frequent phenomena of the Depression years. There were nearly 300 reported kidnappings in 1932, and it was widely believed that the real number was much higher since most kidnappings probably went unreported, possibly because the families feared police involvement.

Americans eagerly turned their attention from their own ongoing misery to the sensational news coming out of New Jersey.

THE INVESTIGATION

LINDBERGH TAKES OVER

In all probability, any clues about the identity of the kidnappers that might have been accidentally left on the grounds surrounding the estate were trampled by the media and the mobs, as confusion gave way to chaos. The rural roads leading to the estate were clogged with cars containing the curious who converged on the area. Planes flew overhead, providing sightseers with an aerial view for the price of $2.50.

Eventually the New Jersey State police, headed by Colonel H. Norman Schwarzkopf (the father of General H. Norman Schwarzkopf, the commander of Coalition forces during the 1991 Gulf War), did secure the area, restricting the media to an area at the far end of the grounds.

Colonel Schwarzkopf was a former army officer with no police training previous to his being named the head of the state police. He and his men had little experience with proper police procedures, and it showed.

He refused to use bloodhounds or the student body of nearby Princeton University to help search the surrounding area for clues. The state police failed to make a cast of or accurately measure the one relatively distinct footprint that was found. Schwarzkopf turned down offers of help from other police agencies, including the New York City police and the Federal Bureau of Investigation. And he was reluctant to share information with them. By refusing the help of the FBI (with some justification, Schwarzkopf considered the FBI and their publicity-conscious director, J. Edgar Hoover, glory hunters), Schwarzkopf forfeited access to the

Bureau's extensive crime-solving facilities and experience (kidnapping was not a federal offense at the time, and the FBI had no jurisdiction in the case). Lindbergh refused to see Hoover when he came to New Jersey.

Schwarzkopf did set up a communications center in the Lindberghs' three-car garage and had a twenty-line switchboard installed. He assigned his troopers to the task of sorting the thousands of letters that had begun arriving. Some offered sympathy and suggestions, others death threats and phony ransom demands. His men questioned everyone who lived in the area, as well as people who worked at bus and railroad stations, taxi companies, and airfields, in hopes that they had seen something suspicious.

While their garage had been converted into a communications center, the Lindberghs' home had become the primary headquarters for the investigation. In fact, Schwarzkopf, in awe of the aviation hero, had allowed Lindbergh to take command of the operation from the beginning.

The police held meetings in the bedrooms and conferred on the stairways, while Lindbergh and his family, household staff, friends, and advisors came and went.

> This house is bedlam: hundreds of men stamping in and out, sitting everywhere, on the stairs, on the pantry sink. The telephone goes all day and night. People sleep all over the floors on newspapers and blankets. I have never seen such self-sacrifice and energy. [Colonel Schwarzkopf] has not been to bed or to rest since the thing started . . . The press have moved down to Hopewell and are not photographing around the place any more. Which allows us to go out and

WANTED

INFORMATION AS TO THE WHEREABOUTS OF

CHAS. A. LINDBERGH, Jr.

OF HOPEWELL, N. J.

SON OF COL. CHAS. A. LINDBERGH

World-Famous Aviator

This child was kidnaped from his home in Hopewell, N. J., between 8 and 10 p. m. on Tuesday, March 1, 1932.

DESCRIPTION:

Age, 20 months	Hair, blond, curly
Weight, 27 to 30 lbs.	Eyes, dark blue
Height, 29 inches	Complexion, light

Deep dimple in center of chin
Dressed in one-piece coverall night suit

ADDRESS ALL COMMUNICATIONS TO
COL. H. N. SCHWARZKOPF, TRENTON, N. J., or
COL. CHAS. A. LINDBERGH, HOPEWELL, N. J.

ALL COMMUNICATIONS WILL BE TREATED IN CONFIDENCE

COL. H. NORMAN SCHWARZKOPF
March 11, 1932   Supt. New Jersey State Police, Trenton, N. J.

Although Col. Schwarzkopf let Lindbergh handle most of the investigation, he did issue this poster.

walk. That is a great help to me . . . There are planes
overhead now.

— Anne Morrow Lindbergh

Lindbergh insisted on speaking to anyone who claimed
to have information about his son. He had purposely with-
held details about certain physical characteristics of the child
from the public so he could be sure if someone had indeed
spotted him. No one had.

He further insisted on making all decisions regarding
communication with the kidnappers. His number-one priority was getting his son back alive. He was concerned that
the police might cause the kidnappers to do something rash.
He didn't want Schwarzkopf to interfere in any way until
the baby was safe. Schwarzkopf, aware that he was dealing
with America's most revered hero, agreed.

Like many others, Lindbergh believed that the kidnapping was the work of professional criminals. Al Capone —
the most famous gangster of the time — agreed with
Lindbergh. Capone was about to begin serving an eleven-
year sentence for income tax evasion. He offered to find the
child in exchange for his freedom. In fact, there were rumors that Capone himself was behind the kidnapping —
which he had supposedly engineered so he could negotiate
his own release. Lindbergh was eager to pursue this theory
but federal authorities were able to convince him that
Capone was bluffing and, in reality, knew nothing.

Lindbergh issued a press release naming Morris "Mickey"
Rosner, a known gangster, to act as an intermediary
between himself and the kidnappers. Rosner set up his
headquarters in the Lindbergh house while his men set
up another base of operations in a New York bar. He was

given a copy of the ransom note to help him make contact.

The Lindberghs also issued a press release giving the details of the baby's diet in hope that the kidnappers would follow it. The diet appeared on the front page of nearly every newspaper in the country the morning of March 3:

> Mrs. Anne Morrow Lindbergh asks that the baby's diet be adhered to, as follows:
> A half cup of orange juice on waking.
> One quart of milk during the day.
> Three tablespoons of cooked cereal morning and night.
> Two tablespoons of cooked vegetables once a day.
> The yolk of one egg daily.
> One baked potato or rice once a day.
> Two tablespoons of stewed fruit daily.
> A half cup of prune juice after the afternoon nap.
> Fourteen drops of viosterol, a vitamin preparation, during the day.

The next day another message from the Lindberghs appeared in the papers:

> Mrs. Lindbergh and I desire to make a personal contact with the kidnapers of our child.
> Our only interest is in his immediate and safe return and we feel certain that the kidnapers will realize that this interest is strong enough to justify them in having complete confidence and trust in any promises that we may make in connection with his return.
> We urge those who have the child to select any rep-

resentative of ours who will be suitable to them at any time and at any place that they may designate.

If this is accepted, we promise that we will keep whatever arrangements that may be made by their representative and ours strictly confidential and we further pledge ourselves that we will not try to injure in any way those connected with the return of the child.

Charles A. Lindbergh
Anne Lindbergh

New Jersey's attorney general, William A. Stevens, issued a statement that contradicted the Lindberghs' apparent offer of immunity. New Jersey, he said, would prosecute those responsible for the crime, regardless of any promises from Lindbergh. This lack of communication and coordination among the authorities was to become characteristic of the entire investigation.

That same day, March 4, the Lindberghs received in the mail a message from the kidnappers. The note warned Lindbergh not to notify the police and said they would have to wait until everything was quiet. A subsequent note assured Lindbergh that the baby was in good health and informed him that the ransom was now $70,000.

That was it.

It had been over a week since the kidnapping. Messages had been exchanged but contact had not been made, negotiations had not begun. Lindbergh was eager to hand over the ransom money and get his son back. But first, someone would have to establish direct contact with the kidnappers.

On March 9, 1932, that person called Charles Lindbergh.

"JAFSIE" AND "GRAVEYARD JOHN"

The caller was John F. Condon, a seventy-two-year-old retired teacher, principal, and athletic coach. He lived in the Bronx, a borough of New York City. Those who liked him considered him somewhat of a character. Those who didn't considered him a bore who talked too much, especially about himself.

Condon considered himself deeply patriotic and, as such, was outraged by what had happened to America's most beloved hero. He wrote a letter to the *Bronx Home News* (circulation 100,000), which had printed many of Condon's letters in the past, offering to act as a go-between.

I offer all I can scrape together so a loving mother may again have her child and Col. Lindbergh may know that the American people are grateful for the honor bestowed upon them by his pluck and daring.

Let the kidnappers know that no testimony of mine, or information coming from me, will be used against them.

I offer $1,000 which I have saved from my salary as additional to the suggested ransom of $50,000 which is said to have been demanded by Col. Lindbergh.

I stand ready at my own expense to go anywhere, alone, to give the kidnapper the extra money and promise never to utter his name to any person.

If this is not agreeable, then I ask the kidnappers to go to any Catholic priest and return the child unharmed, with the knowledge that any priest must hold inviolate any statement which may be made by the kidnappers.

Surprisingly, Condon received a positive reply from the kidnappers the next day.

Condon called and eventually spoke to Lindbergh, who was skeptical at first. But when Condon told him about the odd circles that appeared on the bottom of the note addressed to him (the circles that matched the ones on the original ransom note) Lindbergh became convinced that Condon was in contact with the real kidnappers.

Lindbergh had never divulged the existence of the strange symbols to the media, believing that that would enable him to know when he was in fact dealing with the people who had his son. However, "Mickey" Rosner, the man Lindbergh had originally named as a go-between, had been given a copy of the ransom note. Therefore, the appearance of the symbols didn't completely rule out the possibility that Condon was dealing with extortionists who were attempting to cash in on the kidnapping but actually had no idea where the baby was.

Lindbergh invited Condon to Hopewell, where he arrived about midnight. Condon and Lindbergh talked, and Lindbergh became convinced that Condon was reliable. Before going to bed Condon insisted on meeting Mrs. Lindbergh, who had to be awakened. Condon assured her he would return her child unharmed. That night Condon slept on the floor of the nursery — the only available room. Condon and Lindbergh agreed that a note should be issued by the Lindberghs stating that Condon was authorized to act as a go-between and that the message "money is ready" should be placed in the *New York American*, as the kidnappers had instructed. They also agreed that the media mustn't learn that Condon was an intermediary. To disguise his role, Condon decided to sign the message "Jafsie" because of his initials J.F.C.

The message ran Friday, March 11. That night one of the kidnappers called "Jafsie" at home. Speaking with an accent, he told Condon he had seen the message. It sounded as if he was speaking in Italian to someone standing next to him, ordering them to "shut up." After telling Condon that he would hear from him, the caller hung up.

The next night a note was delivered to Condon by a cab driver.

Although the money wasn't ready, Condon followed the instructions, which led him to a cemetery. After waiting for fifteen minutes he noticed a man in the cemetery waving a handkerchief. When Condon reached the man, who wore a hat and an overcoat and held the handkerchief over his face, he asked Condon if he had the money. Condon said he could not hand over the money until he was sure about the baby. Their conversation was interrupted by a cemetery guard who happened by and frightened the kidnapper. Now agitated, the kidnapper asked Condon if he would "burn" if the baby was dead. This, in turn, agitated Condon, but the kidnapper assured him that the baby was safe and in good health. Condon, however, insisted on proof. The kidnapper, who said his name was John, told Condon he would send the bedclothes the boy was sleeping in that night as proof.

On Wednesday the sleeping suit arrived at Condon's home.

The following week Condon placed a number of messages in the paper, but they went unanswered. Finally, on Monday, March 21, Jafsie heard from the man they'd come to call "Graveyard John." And, a week later he received another note, complaining that the investigation was following what the writer of the note called "false clues."

The "false clues" Graveyard John mentioned involved one of the other leads Lindbergh was following. Although it turned out to be nothing but a cruel hoax, the twists and turns of this other contact with the "kidnappers" received a lot of press. This press coverage was noticed by Graveyard John, who was apparently angry that Lindbergh doubted he was the real kidnapper.

If all this wasn't complicated enough, Lindbergh was still working with Rosner, who continued to claim he was about to make contact with the kidnappers.

On Tuesday, March 31, Jafsie heard from Graveyard John.

John had no intention of giving the baby to Jafsie in direct exchange for the money. Condon wanted to insist that the exchange be made right then and there, but Lindbergh overruled him. Schwarzkopf suggested that John be followed, but Lindbergh vetoed this idea, too.

On Saturday, April 2, Jafsie placed a message that said everything was ready. That night, once again, a cab driver delivered a note to Condon's home:

Dear Sir: take a car and follow tremont Ave to the east until you reach the number 3225 tremont ave.

It is a nursery.

Bergen

Greenhauses florist

ther is a table standing outside right on the door, you find a letter undernead the table covert with a stone, read and follow instruction.

don't speak to anyone on the way. If there is a ratio

alarm for policecar, we warn you, we have the same eqipnent. have the money in one bundle. We give you ¾ of a houer to reach the place.

Lindbergh and Condon drove to the spot where a note was found, directing Condon to another cemetery. Lindbergh waited in the car, while Condon approached the cemetery.

A voice called out, "Hey, Doctor, over here." It was Graveyard John. Condon tried to insist that John take him to the baby, but John refused. After a certain amount of negotiation, Condon gave John the money and John gave Condon a note that told him where he could find the baby. Back in the car he and Lindbergh read the note.

The boy is on the Boad Nelly. It is a small boad 28 feet long. Two persons are on the boad. They are innosent. you will find the Boad between Horseneck Beach and gay Head near Elizabeth Island.

But there was no "Boad Nelly" and there was no baby.

Then, on May 12, 1932, seventy-two days after the kidnapping, the search for the Lindbergh baby ended. A trucker, stopping on a road near the Lindbergh estate, discovered the badly decomposed body of what appeared to be a baby. It was lying facedown in the woods; there was a burlap bag lying nearby.

An examination showed that the child had died from a fractured skull two or three months earlier. It appeared that he had been dead since the night of the kidnapping.

Lindbergh identified the boy, saying only "That is my son."

Friday, May 13, 1932. He has already been dead a
hundred years.

A long sleepless night with [Charles] sitting beside me
every hour, and I could see it all from a great distance. . . .

Then a long day when everything personal flooded
back over me, a personal physical loss, my little boy —
no control over tears, no control over the hundred little incidents I had jammed out of sight when I was
bargaining for my control . . .

I am glad that I spoiled him that last weekend when
he was sick and I took him on my lap and rocked him
and sang to him. And glad that he wanted me those
last days . . .

Impossible to talk without crying.

— Anne Morrow Lindbergh

Lindbergh continued to devote all his time and energy to
the investigation. As long as there had been a chance the
child was alive, the police had followed his instructions.
Now that would change. The search for the Lindbergh baby
was over. The hunt for his killer began.

VIOLET SHARPE

The New Jersey State police didn't think the kidnapping
had been done by professional criminals. Too many things
led them to believe that it was the work of amateurs.

First there was the ransom note. It was crudely written
and awkwardly worded. Clearly the author was foreign-born.
And even if that were a clever ploy designed to hide the real
identity of the kidnappers, the instructions for payment of
the ransom were vague and open-ended. There was no

mention of how or when payment would be made. And then there was the ladder.

Why were the rungs eighteen or nineteen inches apart, rather than the standard twelve inches? This construction made it awkward to use. And when placed against the outside wall below the nursery window, it proved difficult getting from the ladder to the window — but even more difficult getting from the window back to the ladder and descending while holding a thirty-pound child.

The kidnappers had not even taken the fundamental precaution of cutting the phone lines — this was surely not the work of professionals.

No, from the beginning the police had thought the kidnapping was an inside job. That was the only theory that would answer a number of questions.

First, the kidnappers' timing.

It had been perfect — too perfect to be just good luck. The Lindberghs had always stayed at Hopewell on weekends, returning to Englewood every Monday. They had decided to stay over at the last minute. How had the kidnappers known that?

And how had they known when the baby was asleep? The kidnapping had occurred between the time he was usually put to bed and the time he was usually checked on.

The kidnappers had also seemed to know which room the baby was in. Not only that, but they'd seemed to know which of the three windows had the warped shutters that would allow them the easiest access. Perhaps, the police theorized, the warped shutters were no accident. Perhaps they were part of an elaborately conceived plan. All 120 workmen involved in the building of the house were questioned by detectives.

All of the people employed by the Morrows and the Lindberghs were also questioned by the police. At first Lindbergh, who was certain that none of them were involved in the kidnapping, wouldn't even allow Schwarzkopf's men to speak to them. But as the days turned into weeks with the case still unsolved, the police became more insistent. They ran time-consuming background checks on the Morrow and Lindbergh employees (most of whom were from Europe, which complicated matters) and questioned all of them, despite Lindbergh's protests.

Lindbergh's butler and the butler's wife, as well as Betty Gow, were questioned. Red Johnson, Gow's boyfriend, was one of the first to come under suspicion because she had called him the night of the kidnapping. When a milk bottle was discovered in the back of his car after he was picked up for questioning, the police became even more suspicious. But Johnson said he just liked to drink milk when he drove, and the police were never able to find anything linking him to the crime.

Their prime suspect became the Morrows' twenty-seven-year-old English maid, Violet Sharpe. She was the one who answered the phone when Anne Morrow Lindbergh called to ask Betty Gow to come to Hopewell the morning of the kidnapping.

When she was questioned along with the rest of the staff, unlike the others, she refused to cooperate. She told the police that much of what they were asking was none of their business. To the detectives interviewing her, she appeared evasive and defiant.

Then she was caught in a lie. She said she had gone to a movie the night of the kidnapping, but she couldn't remember what it was about or who was in it. Then she changed her story. She hadn't gone to the movies. She had met someone named Ernie (she couldn't remember his last name) and they had gone to a bar together.

In May she went into the hospital to have her tonsils removed. The day after the operation the baby's dead body was discovered. She became depressed. During one interview she collapsed, although the police thought she was faking it.

But there was no question that Violet Sharpe, during the three months of the kidnapping, had gone from a pretty, independent, plump girl to a gaunt, frightened woman who looked older than her years. She had lost over forty pounds.

" . . . Life is getting so sad I really don't think there is much to live for anymore," she wrote in a letter.

On June 9, after she was questioned again by the police, she became hysterical. In front of other members of the Morrow staff she swore she wasn't going to allow herself to be subjected to any more questioning.

At 10:00 A.M. the next day the state police called the Morrow estate to say they were coming to take Violet back to headquarters for another round of questions. When the detectives arrived she went to her room, poured poisonous cyanide (she used the crystals for cleaning the Morrows' silver) into a glass, filled the glass with water, drank the poisonous liquid, and made her way downstairs — where she fell to the floor dead.

The police viewed Violet's suicide as they had viewed her behavior during questioning: as a sign of guilt. Schwarzkopf believed she was the inside contact for the kidnappers.

He issued a public statement that indicated they were looking for "Ernie" and that the case would be solved soon.

It had been more than three months since the kidnapping—one month since the baby had been found dead.
Schwarzkopf and his men were being criticized by the media
for bungling the case.

There was, however, another explanation for Violet's behavior. She was romantically involved with the Morrows'
butler. It was possible that she feared the police investigation, which had already forced her to reveal her date with
Ernie, might also force her to reveal other men she had
known. That information might result in her losing her job
and her relationship with the butler — losses she might well
have considered crushing blows.

Violet's behavior might not have been the result of anything to do with the kidnapping. Her behavior could have
been caused by what she considered badgering by the police — badgering that was threatening to ruin her life.

The day after Violet Sharpe's suicide, Ernest Miller, a
twenty-three-year-old New Jersey bus driver, came forward. He had indeed had a date with Violet the night of the
kidnapping. His story matched hers in every deatil and he
was cleared of any wrongdoing.

No evidence or information of any kind linking Violet
Sharpe to the Lindbergh kidnapping has ever been found.

4U-13-14 N.Y.

When the package of ransom money was being put together, Elmer Irey, head of the Internal Revenue Service's
Enforcement Division, insisted that gold certificates be included. Gold certificates, because of their distinctive round
yellow seal, would be more easily recognized than ordinary

bills. This would insure that if the kidnappers weren't apprehended immediately (which turned out to be the case) the authorities would have a way of tracking them down. Once the kidnappers started spending the money, the trail of where they were spending it might lead to where they lived. Store owners or clerks might be able to give authorities a visual identification. The gold certificates might turn out to be the only hope they had, and Irey was firm on including them.

Lindbergh had objected to this, as he had to other suggestions that he believed might jeopardize his chances of getting his son back alive. But Irey prevailed. It proved to be a critical decision.

Gold certificates became even more conspicuous in April 1933. President Franklin Delano Roosevelt wanted the United States to go off the gold standard, which had governed the nation's currency until then. He signed an executive order that made gold certificates illegal. Americans had until May 1, 1933, to exchange their gold certificates for federal reserve notes. Failure to comply could mean a ten-thousand-dollar fine and/or ten years in jail.

Gold certificates made up more than half the ransom money and their serial numbers had been recorded. They had become the authorities' best chance for solving the two-year-old crime.

Only days after Condon had handed over the ransom money to Graveyard John, a bill with corresponding serial numbers turned up at a New York City bank. Soon other bills began appearing, sporadically, in New York. The money was being spent cautiously, as if the bill passer knew the money was "hot."

However, by late 1933 the pattern became less cautious.

He seemed to be using the money for everyday expenses — the bills were being passed in small stores. The people who worked in these stores were able to give a description of the man who gave them the money. The description matched that given by Condon and Joseph Perrone, the cab driver who had delivered one of the ransom notes to Condon's home. The bill passer was of average height and weight, had light hair, was about forty years old, and spoke with a German accent. He always took the bills out of his vest or trouser watch pocket and then casually threw them on the counter. They were always folded in the same peculiar manner: once lengthwise and then twice more. The shopkeepers invariably commented about having to flatten out the bill in order to see the denomination.

In one particular case, a cashier at a Manhattan movie theater remembered the man who used a folded five-dollar gold certificate to pay for a 55-cent movie ticket. She confirmed the description others had given to the New York City police.

Further study of the bills revealed more. They had an odor, as if they had been buried in a cellar or another damp, moldy place. Traces of emery, a granular substance, were also found. This could mean that the man passing the bills was someone who sharpened his own tools — a carpenter, for instance. A carpenter who could make his own ladder.

New York City banks had received a 57-page booklet listing the serial numbers of the Lindbergh ransom money. They were urged to watch carefully for them. That was easier said than done, however. The booklet was difficult to use, because it was lengthy and the columns of small type were hard to read. Bank officials and the police had a difficult time tracing the bills to specific deposits.

New York Police Department detectives, led by Detective James Finn, responded to every sighting, and urged the bank personnel to continue their efforts. They also offered a five-dollar reward for any ransom money discovered.

Finn had been tracing the location of the bills since April 1932, when they first began to appear. Each time one was discovered, a pin was stuck into a large map of New York City that was mounted on the wall at police headquarters. At first the bill passer seemed to be making an effort not to spend the money in any particular area. After a while, however, the pins began to be clustered in the area around the cemetery where Jafsie had met Graveyard John.

Because of this and the fact that the kidnapper had responded to Jafsie's ad in the *Bronx Home News*, Finn assumed that he lived in the Bronx. He speculated that the kidnapper probably had a car. If the kidnapper was spending the ransom money for things like fruit, vegetables, shoes, and movies, then he would use it to buy gas for his car. Finn asked all filling stations in New York State to record the license number of any vehicle whose driver paid for gas with gold certificates.

On Tuesday, September 18, 1934, Finn's diligence paid off. A ten-dollar gold certificate with a serial number that matched those assigned to the Lindbergh ransom money had turned up in a bank in the Bronx. The marked bill had *4U-13-14 N.Y.* written in the margin. Finn was sure it was a New York State license plate number that had been noted by an alert attendant. There was a gas station a few blocks away from the bank.

The owner of the gas station and his attendant told Finn that three days earlier a man driving a blue Dodge had bought 98 cents' worth of gas with a ten-dollar gold certifi-

The ten-dollar ransom bill passed by Hauptmann at the Warner-Quinlan gas station. An attendant penciled Hauptmann's license plate number in the left margin on the back of the bill.

cate. The attendant had written the license plate number on the bill before he drove away. The man spoke with a German accent.

The license was traced through the New York Motor Vehicles Bureau. The 1930 Dodge belonged to Bruno Richard Hauptmann of East 222nd Street in the Bronx. The address was near the cemetery where Jafsie had given Graveyard John the ransom money.

A FISCH STORY

Finn decided not to arrest Hauptmann at home. For one thing, he might be armed. But more importantly, if they caught him outside, he might be in possession of the ransom money.

The next morning, September 19, 1934, Hauptmann pulled his blue Dodge (license plate number 4U-13-14) out of the one-car garage adjacent to his hime. After following him for a couple of miles, the police, fearing that they might lose him in the traffic, surrounded his car and arrested him. In his wallet they found a twenty-dollar gold certificate.

Anna, Hauptmann's wife, was stunned to see her husband in the custody of the police, who began to search their apartment. They found road maps of New Jersey, binoculars, and a notebook containing a drawing of a ladder and

Crowds gathered outside Hauptmann's home in the Bronx shortly after his arrest.

two windows. Five days later, on the wall of the closet in their eleven-month-old son's room, the police found something written in pencil. It appeared that someone had tried to rub it out, but it could still be read: *2974 Decatur* and *3-7154-SDG*. The first was Jafsie's address and the second, his telephone number.

While they were searching the apartment, the detectives noticed Hauptmann stealing glances out the window in the direction of the garage. The garage was then thoroughly searched and over $14,000 of the Lindbergh ransom money was found, hidden in various places.

Hauptmann had been taken to a police station while the garage was being searched. He was questioned incessantly by a revolving team of detectives who forced him to sit in a

Investigators tear up Hauptmann's garage as they hunt for evidence.

After hours of questioning, Hauptmann was moved from the Greenwich Street Station House to the Bronx County Courthouse.

chair for the first seven hours without moving, drinking, or eating. He was denied sleep for three days — other than dozing off from time to time in between interrogation sessions. At one point he was beaten with a blunt instrument.

He said he didn't know anything about the Lindbergh ransom money, and that he couldn't remember what he was doing on Tuesday evening, March 1, 1932 — the night of the kidnapping.

His wife was questioned separately and she, too, denied knowing anything about the kidnapping. She said she couldn't remember where her husband was that night — it was too long ago.

When Hauptmann was confronted by the evidence the police had uncovered in his garage, he admitted having the money but said he had lied about it because it was illegal to possess gold certificates, not because he had anything to do with the kidnapping. Asked to explain how he had gotten the money, Hauptmann told the police about Isidore Fisch.

He told the police that Fisch, a fellow German immigrant, had given him the money. He had met Fisch in April 1932 (the same month the ransom money had been given to Graveyard John). They had become partners in the fur business, eventually making over $10,000.

In December 1933, Fisch had asked Hauptmann if he would hold some of his things while Fisch visited his family in Germany. Hauptmann had agreed, and one of the things Fisch had given him was a cardboard shoe box tied with string. Hauptmann said he had put it in the closet and hadn't given it another thought until two weeks earlier. At that time the closet had leaked after a heavy rainstorm and the shoe box had gotten wet. When he had opened it he saw, much to his surprise, that it was filled with money. At first he had hidden the money in the garage, but then he had decided to spend some of it. He had felt justified in doing this because Fisch had owed him money from a loan that he had never repaid.

Asked where they could find Fisch, Hauptmann told the police that he had died of tuberculosis on March 29, 1934, while still in Germany.

The police checked Hauptmann's Fisch story. Fisch had indeed gone to Germany when Hauptmann said he had — in fact he applied for his passport on May 12, 1932, the same day the Lindbergh baby's body was discovered. And the police found that Hauptmann was right, Fisch was dead.

The police also ran a check on Hauptmann. He was born

Bruno Hauptmann photographed at New Jersey State Police Headquarters, where a criminal file on him was opened.

in 1899 and had served time in jail for armed robbery. One incident involved burglarizing a home by using a ladder to enter a second-story window. In 1923 Hauptmann had come illegally to America and worked as a dishwasher, a mechanic, and, finally, a carpenter.

The detectives continued to press Hauptmann, who stuck to his Fisch story and denied any involvement with the kidnapping. They asked him if he would be willing to take a handwriting test and he eagerly agreed. He said he would like to do anything that would prove his innocence.

The test had been designed by Albert S. Osborn, Sr., the police handwriting expert. The words in the test contained many of the misspelled words found in the ransom notes. The police dictated for hours on end while Hauptmann wrote page after page of dictation, finally collapsing, exhausted.

Hauptmann was then extradited from New York, where he had been arrested, to New Jersey, where the crime had been committed. In New Jersey he would stand trial for murder.

THE TRIAL

CARNIVAL

The formerly quiet town of Flemington, New Jersey (pop. 2,700 including two policemen), was overrun by hundreds

A mob scene outside the Flemington Courthouse.

of reporters, radio personalities, celebrities (singers, sports figures, movie stars, comedians, and famous writers), and thousands of sightseers who came to see the trial, which began on January 2, 1935.

Twenty thousand cars brought an estimated sixty thousand people into the area. Traffic on the roads leading into Flemington was backed up for ten miles in every direction, moving — when it moved at all — at a rate of three miles an hour. Cars were parked anywhere, as their occupants headed for Main Street and the courthouse. The local authorities were overwhelmed by the crowds, which rushed past them and wreaked havoc inside the courtroom. They swarmed over everything: sat in the judge's chair, posed for pictures on the witness stand, carved their initials wherever they could, and took anything that might be considered a souvenir (including soap and toilet paper) —sometimes fighting over it, and generally acting like fools. After the first weekend the courthouse was closed to visitors.

More media attention was focused on the Hauptmann trial than any previous event in American history. There were reporters representing nearly every paper in the United States, and one news organization sent fifty. A network of telephone and telegraph wires ran in and out of the courthouse windows, up the walls, and across the floors. Half a million words a day flowed out of Flemington to an eager, waiting world.

For many of the townspeople the trial was proving to be good news financially. Those who had spare rooms (and in some cases families doubled up on sleeping arrangements so they did) rented them at sky-high prices. Flemington's only hotel was booked solid. Their fifty rooms had been taken even before the trial started and they had to turn down

News syndicates and special correspondents set up wire rooms like this one at the Union Hotel in Flemington.

hundreds of requests. (Six rooms had been reserved for the jury.) Extra staff had been hired so the dining room could stay open until midnight. Those unable to find room in Flemington commuted from Trenton or from New York City.

Flemington looked more like a carnival than a town. Flashbulbs popped as celebrities came and went, eager to be seen at what had become the fashionable place to be: the "Trial of the Century," as it was called.

Scale models of the kidnap ladder (ten cents), "locks of the baby's hair" (five dollars), and "signed" photographs of Charles and Anne Lindbergh were being sold at a brisk pace. Women considered it stylish to pin the little ladders to their lapels.

Inside the courthouse, corridors were clogged with media people and hangers-on. The overheated, poorly ventilated courtroom, which would have had trouble holding 200 people, now held twice that many. The public was seated on a first-come, first-served basis. Every seat, every space, was taken as people jostled for position. Scalpers were getting as much as $500 a ticket for reserved seats.

The judge was seventy-one-year-old Thomas Trenchard. This would be the ninety-second murder trial he would preside over. The prosecution was led by New Jersey's young attorney general, David Wilentz. This was his first criminal trial. The defense team was headed by fifty-two-year-old Edward Reilly.

"Big Ed" Reilly had built a reputation for getting his clients acquitted in difficult homicide cases. Reilly had become Hauptmann's lawyer when Anna Hauptmann agreed

Ignoring the seriousness of the trial taking place just a few yards away, young boys sold miniature replicas of the kidnap ladder, which became fashionable souvenirs.

Prosecutor David T. Wilentz (left) with his star witness, John "Jafsie" Condon.

to a proposal from the Hearst newspaper organization. They would pay Reilly's hefty fee in exchange for exclusive rights to her story — including covering her visits to her husband in his jail cell. Anna, concerned about her husband and impressed with Reilly's record, agreed. It was a tragic mistake.

The flamboyant, pompous Reilly was eccentric and old-fashioned to a degree bordering on the absurd. He wore formal attire while trying the case: a cutaway morning coat, gray-striped trousers, spats, and a white carnation in his lapel — not the kind of clothes or attitude to win the hearts and minds of a rural New Jersey jury.

Reilly was at one time considered a top criminal lawyer. But he was past his prime, had been married four times, and was an alcoholic. He took the case only because of the publicity it would bring him. In keeping with the carnival atmosphere he had stationery printed up with *The Lind-*

Hauptmann's wife, Anna, with his lawyer, "Big Ed" Reilly.

bergh-Hauptmann *Trial* on the top and a ladder drawn in red ink running down the side of the page. Throughout the trial he evidenced little real interest in the case or in his client and spent little time with Hauptmann either before or during the trial.

THE EYEWITNESSES

Charles and Anne Lindbergh were among the first to testify. Anne told about the events the night of the kidnapping and identified the baby's nightclothes.

Reilly declined to question her. "The defense feels that the grief of Mrs. Lindbergh requires no cross-examination," he said.

Charles testified that he was certain it was Hauptmann's

A rare photograph of Anne Morrow Lindbergh on the witness stand.

voice he had heard say "Hey, Doctor, over here" that night outside the cemetery:

> "I heard very clearly a voice coming from the cemetery, to the best of my belief calling Dr. Condon."
> Wilentz asked, "What were these words?"
> "In a foreign accent: 'Hey, Doctor.'"
> "Since that time have you heard the same voice?"
> "Yes, I have."
> Wilentz waited a moment.
> "Whose voice was it, Colonel, that you heard calling, 'Hey, Doctor?'"
> "That was Hauptmann's voice," Charles said decisively.

Lindbergh's identification of Hauptmann, made as he looked right at him, was crucial to the state's case. Anne returned to the courtroom only once, to accompany her mother when she testified about Violet Sharpe. Lindbergh attended every day, sitting three seats from Hauptmann, who was flanked by New Jersey State troopers.

Lindbergh on the stand. Later, some jurors would say that his testimony was pivotal in influencing their decision.

The cab driver who had been given the note to deliver to Condon's home identified Hauptmann, as did the cashier at the movie theater where Hauptmann was alleged to have paid for his ticket with a five-dollar ransom bill. The cashier's testimony was important because November 26, 1933 — the date she said Hauptmann had gone to the movies — was a month before Fisch had sailed for Germany and therefore *before* he had given Hauptmann the shoe box full of money, as Hauptmann said he had. If the cashier was correct, then Hauptmann was lying.

Ben Lupica, a student, testified that he saw Hauptmann with a ladder in his car near the Lindbergh estate. Millard Whited and eighty-seven-year-old Amandus Hochmuth, two neighbors, also testified that they had seen Hauptmann in the area. Hochmuth told the court that he had been sitting on his front porch the day of the kidnapping when he saw Hauptmann drive by in a car with a ladder in it.

But perhaps the most important eyewitness was John F. Condon — Jafsie — the man who had met twice with

Graveyard John. His testimony was eagerly anticipated, in part because of the fireworks many thought the Reilly-Condon encounter would give off— it was billed as the Battle of the Blustering Bulls. Condon had revealed himself as somewhat of a buffoon over the past two years. There was no question that, despite the fact that he had failed in his mission, he thoroughly enjoyed the publicity that surrounded his every move and utterance. Now he would have his day in the courtroom — which was packed. He didn't disappoint the crowd. In a thundering voice he proclaimed that the man he'd met in the cemetery, the man to whom he had given the ransom money, was Bruno Richard Hauptmann.

THE EXPERTS

Even more damning than the eyewitnesses was the testimony of two of the prosecution's expert witnesses.

Albert Osborn, Sr., was the country's most highly regarded handwriting expert. Patiently, using a pointer, he explained to the jury what he saw in the photographic enlargements displaying the letters and words in Hauptmann's handwriting and those taken from the ransom notes.

Osborn pointed out the similarities. Words misspelled a particular way by Hauptmann were misspelled the same way in the ransom notes: "mony" (money); "boad" (boat); "anyding" (anything); "lihgt" (light); "rihgt" (right); "not" (note); "gut" (good).

Of the nearly 400 *t*'s in the ransom notes only three were crossed. Of the 300 *i*'s only seven were dotted. The same percentage of crossed to uncrossed *t*'s and dotted to undotted *i*'s appeared in the handwriting samples Hauptmann

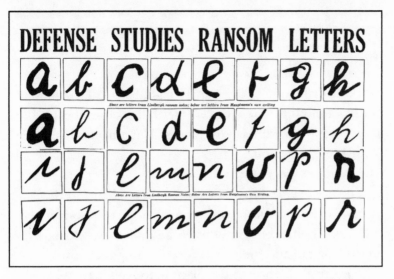

DEFENSE STUDIES RANSOM LETTERS

Above are letters from Lindbergh ransom notes; below are letters from Hauptmann's own writing

Above Are Letters from Lindbergh Ransom Notes; Below Are Letters from Hauptmann's Own Writing.

At the trial, the prosecution exhibited handwriting samples like this one comparing Hauptmann's writing with that of the ransom notes.

produced when he was being interrogated by the police after his arrest.

The evidence was clear and convincing, as far as Osborn was concerned: Hauptmann had written the ransom notes.

The prosecution believed that Osborn's testimony showed that Hauptmann had written the ransom notes, but that didn't mean he had kidnapped the baby. To make that link the state called Arthur Koehler.

Koehler was a wood technologist for the U.S. Department of Agriculture. He was a well-known authority on wood — the author of a book and a number of articles on the subject.

Like Osborn, Koehler made use of a number of displays to illustrate his testimony. He had, he explained, traced the wood used to construct the ladder found the night of the kidnapping to trees grown in South Carolina. From there he traced the wood to the mill where it was planed. Under the lens of his microscope Koehler had detected a slight mark made by one of the planer's eight blades. That allowed him to follow the wood from the mill to a lumberyard in the Bronx — a lumberyard where Hauptmann had been known to buy wood.

And there was more.

Koehler believed that one piece of the side rail of the ladder had originally been used somewhere else — somewhere indoors. Koehler believed this because there were nail holes in the side rail and the holes showed no signs of rust.

Detectives discovered the place indoors where the wood had originally been — Hauptmann's attic. Koehler testified that the piece of wood still in Hauptmann's attic floor and the side rail of the ladder used in the kidnapping had originally been one and the same. The nail holes in the side rail matched those in the attic flooring and the wood grain in both was the same. Hauptmann, according to Koehler, having run out of wood while building the ladder, had sawed the piece he needed from the attic floor. According to Koehler, Hauptmann, a carpenter by trade, had built the crude but cleverly conceived ladder. A ladder that was both lightweight and — when taken apart — would fit into a car that could then transport it to the scene of the crime.

Koehler's testimony, although complicated and at times tedious and difficult to follow, made a lasting impression on the jury. Koehler might just as well have been driving the nails into Hauptmann's coffin.

On January 24, 1935, the prosecution rested.

THE DEFENSE

The courtroom was crowded and noisy when Bruno Richard Hauptmann took the stand.

He testified that he had been working as a carpenter at the Majestic Apartments in New York City on the day of the kidnapping and the night the ransom money was transferred. He said he had not gone to the movies on November 26, 1933 (which happened to be his birthday), that he had misspelled the words in the handwriting samples because the police forced him to write them down exactly that way, that he hadn't built that ladder, that the Fisch story was true, and that he knew nothing about the Lindbergh kidnapping other than what he had read in the papers.

The prosecution disputed Hauptmann's claim that he had been at work on March 1 and April 2. They presented records that showed he hadn't started work until March 21, and hadn't worked on April 2. Wilentz also produced notebooks found in Hauptmann's apartment that showed he had misspelled some of the same words years before the kidnapping. The words, the prosecution insisted, weren't misspelled because the police had forced him to write them down that way. The words were misspelled the same way

A film cameraman captured one of the most dramatic moments of the trial as Hauptmann protested the accusations made by the prosecution.

they were in the ransom notes because that was the way Hauptmann had always spelled those words. Hauptmann was, the prosecution insisted, the author of the ransom notes.

Hauptmann, speaking hesitantly in English, his second language, testified for seventeen hours — eleven of them while being cross-examined by Wilentz.

Anna took the stand next. She told the court that her husband always picked her up on Tuesday nights at the bakery where she worked. The owner of the bakery and his wife confirmed what Anna said, but neither could swear to having seen him on that *particular* Tuesday night, the night of the kidnapping.

All the witnesses called by Reilly in Hauptmann's defense were either poorly prepared or completely discredited by Wilentz. Many were clearly questionable. Reilly had, in one of his many foolish decisions, made a public radio appeal for witnesses to come forward to help Hauptmann. The jury, rightly in some cases, saw them as unbelievable. Hauptmann, also rightly, saw that they were hurting his case.

THE VERDICT

Wilentz's summation lasted five hours. He even had a theory about the peculiar, blue-and-red colored symbols that appeared on the bottom of the ransom notes: the interlocking circles with holes punched in them. Blue was for Bruno, red was for Richard, and the holes were for Hauptmann.

After twenty-nine days of testimony the jury retired to deliberate.

The jury who sentenced Hauptmann to death. They deliberated for only a little more than eleven hours.

A little over eleven hours later, the courthouse bell tolled — the traditional signal that the jury had reached a verdict and was returning.

Hauptmann, chained to his guards, was brought in from his cell. The crowd outside had been chanting "Kill Hauptmann" throughout the day and into the night.

Asked if they had reached a verdict, the jury said they had. They found Bruno Richard Hauptmann guilty of murder in the first degree. They did not recommend leniency, which meant, by law, he would be put to death.

After more than a year of complicated and desperate appeals, which included the U.S. Supreme Court's refusal to consider the case and the intervention of the governor of New Jersey, who had expressed doubts about the verdict, a date was set for Hauptmann's execution. At 8:44 on the evening of April 3, 1936, Hauptmann, his head shaved and his right pant leg torn, was strapped into the electric chair at the New Jersey State prison at Trenton. Three minutes later he was pronounced dead.

JUSTICE?

There were few Americans in 1936, the year Hauptmann was executed, who even considered the possibility that he was innocent. In five years America would be at war with Germany, and anti-German feelings were already beginning to swell. Hauptmann, a German who spoke English with an accent, was considered by most to be guilty as charged.

But in the years since, questions have been raised about the investigation, the trial, and the verdict.

There is little question but that Edward Reilly did a poor job of defending his client. His strategy — to convince the jury that the kidnapping had been an inside job — failed. His attempts to cast suspicion on Betty Gow, Elsie Whately (one of the Lindberghs' housekeepers), and Violet Sharpe fell on deaf ears.

Even worse was his attempt to convince the jury that the baby had been killed by Lindbergh's neighbors — neighbors who were angry that his new home had cut them off from a road they frequently used (in fact, it hadn't).

Reilly failed to challenge critical testimony and appeared to have little belief in his client's innocence. (He called him Bruno — a name Hauptmann disliked and didn't use. His wife and friends called him Richard.) Having his fee paid by the Hearst organization was, at best, a conflict of interest. The Hearst papers made no secret of their belief that Hauptmann was guilty.

Reilly's performance was, at times, foolish and, at times, incompetent. Two years after the trial he entered an insane asylum.

There is reason to believe that many of those who testified for the prosecution were coerced by the police or lied for their own reasons.

Millard Whited originally told the police he hadn't seen anything. After Hauptmann was arrested and Whited learned of the $25,000 reward (he eventually received $1,000), he claimed he had seen Hauptmann in the area. His neighbors considered Whited a liar.

Elderly Amandus Hochmuth, another eyewitness who said he had seen Hauptmann in the area, was also questionable. He was considered crazy by some of his neighbors and had cataracts in both eyes, causing partial blindness. (In 1937, Hochmuth, at a hearing about the reward money — he eventually received $150 — identified a cabinet with flowers on it as a woman wearing a hat.)

The cashier at the movie theater had identified Hauptmann as the murderer of the Lindbergh baby after she had seen his picture in the papers. Like others, she remembered that the bill used to pay for the ticket was folded into eight sections. If Hauptmann was the man she had seen that night, it is reasonable to assume that the bill he used to pay for his gas and any other ransom money found on him would be folded in a similar fashion. Unfortunately historians vary on this point. Some say that at the time of his arrest the ransom bill found in his wallet was folded. Others disagree, saying it wasn't, and still others fail to mention whether it was folded or not. And, the question arises, why would Hauptmann, on the night of his birthday, go alone to a movie a considerable distance from where he lived?

Joseph Perrone, the cab driver, at first didn't think he could identify the man who had given him the note to deliver. But once Hauptmann was in custody he had no trouble. (Hauptmann, exhausted after hours of interrogation, appeared in a lineup flanked by two taller, clean-shaven, well-dressed policemen.)

Lindbergh also originally said he would have difficulty identifying the voice he heard that night in the cemetery. But by the time of the trial he was sure the voice was Hauptmann's.

The most surprising change of heart was Condon's. He had refused to identify Hauptmann when viewing a police lineup. At the hearing held to determine if Hauptmann could be transferred to New Jersey to stand trial, the prosecution didn't even call Condon as a witness. They were not sure what he would say. But Condon, too, by the time of the trial, had changed his mind. Condon was sure that the man he gave the money to was Hauptmann.

Why did Condon reverse himself?

Some suspect that he was threatened by the police or thought he was. In the two years since the baby's body had been found, Condon had gone from savior to suspect. It is possible that he was pressured by the New Jersey State police and/or the attorney general's office. If he failed to identify Hauptmann he might somehow have been tied to the case and prosecuted.

Questions have also been raised about the reliability of testimony by the prosecution's expert witnesses.

Albert Osborn, Sr.'s, son was also a handwriting expert. He had initially told the police he didn't think Hauptmann had written the ransom notes. But that was before the money discovered in Hauptmann's garage became front-page news. After that, Osborn, Jr., apparently came around to his father's conclusions and had no doubt that Hauptmann had written the ransom notes.

There is also reason to believe that the police may have fabricated some evidence, and doctored and suppressed other pieces of evidence.

First there are the markings found in Hauptmann's son's closet: *2974 Decatur, 3-7154 SDG,* Condon's address and phone number.

During his interrogation Hauptmann admitted he had written the numbers there. He said he had been following the case in the papers. Later, however, he denied writing anything and was sorry he'd said he had. He was not sure what the police were talking about.

It is hard to believe that, if Hauptmann was the man who murdered the Lindbergh baby, he would write down the phone number and address of the man he was negotiating with in a closet in his own house — especially since Hauptmann did not have a phone.

There are those who claim to know who did write Condon's address and phone number in the closet: a journalist covering the case, who had access to the apartment. Anxious to help make certain Hauptmann was found guilty, he may have planted the evidence.

Some records pertaining to Hauptmann's employment history at the Majestic Apartments seem to have been doctored and others to have disappeared. On one form a check (√) was usually placed in a box if someone worked that day. If not, a zero (0) was written in. It appears a check had been placed alongside Hauptmann's name in the box for the day of the kidnapping. But someone had turned the check into a dark blob in order to obscure it. This was not done anywhere else on the forms — all other zeroes were neat and round.

Other records that might have helped Hauptmann's case had disappeared some time between Hauptmann's arrest and the trial.

There are also questions about the piece of wood in the attic floor of Hauptmann's apartment. Numerous policemen had searched the attic many times without discovering anything having to do with the kidnapping. Even the detective who eventually discovered the floorboard that matched the wood in the side rail of the ladder had found nothing during his prior searches. Why this sudden discovery?

Possibly the detectives knew of Koehler's progress in the case — knew that Koehler had concluded that the side rail of the ladder had been part of another, longer piece of wood that had been used indoors. Eager to make sure that the evidence against Hauptmann was overwhelming, the detective might have gone up to the attic, taking with him the piece of side rail with the nail holes. He might have cut off a piece of the floorboard, laid the side rail from the ladder next to it, and hammered the nails through the holes into the adjacent piece of wood flooring. It would now look as if the side rail of the ladder had been part of the floorboard and had been sawed off, when in fact it hadn't.

Why would Hauptmann, who bought wood at a nearby lumberyard, go up to his own attic, rip out a piece of the floorboard, and use that to complete a ladder he was building to kidnap the Lindbergh baby?

Why, if Hauptmann was the kidnapper, would he spend the ransom money in places right around his neighborhood? Why would he go into the gas station, where they could write down his license plate number, and pay for his gas with a conspicuous gold note that was part of the hot ransom money?

There's more — the questions that plagued the police from the beginning. How could Hauptmann have known that the Lindberghs were staying in Hopewell that night? How did Hauptmann know which room was the baby's and at what time he was put to bed?

And last, what happened to the theory that was held by almost everyone involved in the case — the theory that the kidnapping was the work of more than one person. The ransom letters all said "we," and Graveyard John had told Jafsie that there were six in his gang. Jafsie had also heard someone speaking Italian in the background during a telephone conversation with Graveyard John. Once Hauptmann was arrested, the theory disappeared. Suddenly it became a one-man job and that one man was Hauptmann.

Hauptmann never confessed. His silence has helped a number of theories about the kidnapping flourish in the sixty years since the trial.

Some consider Hauptmann a "scapegoat" — an innocent man framed by a frustrated police department, a department that, after two years of being unable to develop a single lead in the most notorious crime of the time, was not about to let him go free.

It is also possible that Hauptmann was not completely innocent. It is possible that Isador Fisch — probably a petty criminal at the time — was involved in the kidnapping. It is hard to believe that it is just a coincidence that Fisch applied for a passport on the day the baby's body was discovered. If Fisch was involved it is possible, maybe even likely, that Hauptmann, in some way, was also.

It is possible that Hauptmann was in fact guilty and

the authorities, eager to insure a conviction, fabricated and tampered with the evidence.

In 1981 and again in 1986, Anna Hauptmann sued the state of New Jersey for unjustly executing her husband. The suit was dismissed. She requested that the governor of New Jersey conduct a new investigation. He refused.

Chapter Nine

*I decided to take my family abroad until conditions in my
own country change enough to let me establish a reasonably
safe and happy home for them.*

— Charles Lindbergh

THE AIRMAIL CONTROVERSY

Between the time their son was kidnapped (1932) and
Hauptmann's execution (1936), the Lindberghs tried to
reestablish their lives.

On August 6, 1932, Jon, their second son, had been
born. They received hundreds of letters threatening to kidnap him, and the media continued to harass them.

The Lindberghs no longer lived in the house they had
built near Hopewell. After the baby's body had been found,
they stayed there only once, during the trial, and never re-

177

turned. (The house and the land were donated to the state of New Jersey for use as a home for children in need.) Charles, Anne, and Jon moved into a separate wing at the Morrows' Englewood estate. State troopers patrolled the grounds and privately hired armed guards supplemented their efforts.

Lindbergh also bought a German shepherd guard dog. Thor (as he was later named) wouldn't, his trainer assured Lindbergh, be friendly to strangers. Charles was pleased when Thor growled at him. He turned out to be protective of the baby and unwilling to leave Anne's side.

Lindbergh continued working with Pan Am and Trans-continental Air Transport (now Trans World Airways, or TWA). He surveyed new routes, helped choose and test landing fields, and worked on the problems of an emerging industry. And he continued as a spokesman for the further-ing of commercial aviation.

In early 1934, Lindbergh became embroiled in a contro-versy over airmail contracts. A congressional committee had been created to investigate possible fraud in the awarding of those contracts.

It was the responsibility of the postmaster general to award the contracts. There was reason to believe that he had secretly made a deal with the big airline companies — an agreement that would effectively squeeze the smaller com-panies out of the bidding process. It was alleged that the deal, made behind closed doors, resulted in the public pay-ing millions more per year for airmail deliveries. Lower bids made by smaller companies were routinely ignored. One contract had been awarded to a large airline company even though their bid was three times higher than that of a smaller company. In fact, the three big airlines won twenty-four of the twenty-seven contracts.

President Roosevelt believed that the contracts had been unfairly awarded. Without waiting for the committee to make its recommendations, on February 9, 1934, he issued an executive order canceling the contracts. The Army Air Corps was asked to take over responsibility for flying the mail. They agreed.

On February 11, 1934, Lindbergh sent a telegram to Roosevelt criticizing his decision.

YOUR ACTION OF YESTERDAY AFFECTS FUNDAMEN-TALLY THE INDUSTRY TO WHICH I HAVE DEVOTED THE LAST TWELVE YEARS OF MY LIFE. THEREFORE I RESPECTIVELY PRESENT TO YOU THE FOLLOWING CONSIDERATIONS. THE PERSONAL AND BUSINESS LIVES OF AMERICAN CITIZENS HAVE BEEN BUILT AROUND THE RIGHT TO JUST TRIAL BEFORE CON-DEMNATION. YOUR ORDER . . . CONDEMNS THE LARGEST PORTION OF OUR COMMERCIAL AVIATION WITHOUT JUST TRIAL . . . YOUR PRESENT ACTION DOES NOT DISCRIMINATE BETWEEN INNOCENCE AND GUILT AND PLACES NO PREMIUM ON HONEST BUSINESS . . . AMERICANS HAVE SPENT THEIR BUSI-NESS LIVES IN BUILDING IN THIS COUNTRY THE FINEST COMMERCIAL AIRLINES IN THE WORLD . . . THE GREATER PART OF THIS PROGRESS HAS BEEN BROUGHT ABOUT THROUGH THE AIR MAIL . . . CONDEMNATION OF COMMERCIAL AVIATION BY CANCELLATION OF ALL MAIL CONTRACTS AND THE

USE OF THE ARMY ON COMMERCIAL AIRLINES WILL
UNNECESSARILY AND GREATLY DAMAGE ALL AMERI-
CAN AVIATION.

Lindbergh was not above using the press when it served
his purposes. He gave the newspapers a copy of the telegram before Roosevelt had a chance to see it. The telegram
attacked Roosevelt for condemning the big airlines without
a fair trial and needlessly endangering the lives of the Air
Corps pilots. Lindbergh, of course, was not an impartial observer. He was employed by Pan Am and TWA, and the lat-
ter had compensated him with $250,000 worth of stock
when he came on board.

The issue was a complicated one. Some, like Lindbergh,
believed that the contracts had been fairly awarded to the
big airlines. And, they added, the small independents were
unsound, in most cases.

Roosevelt, however, didn't appreciate Lindbergh's leak-
ing the telegram, and he believed that Lindbergh was using
his fame to help big business continue to cheat the public.

The Air Corps had no time to prepare and shouldn't have
accepted the assignment. Their pilots had no night flying
experience and their planes lacked the right equipment.
Both pilots and planes were unprepared for the severe winter weather: blizzards, sleet, fog, and frigid cold.

After one week, five pilots had been killed and six seriously injured in eight plane crashes. Within two months,
seven more were dead.

Public opinion, in part due to the deaths of the pilots,
was on Lindbergh's side. Roosevelt was forced to give the
airmail routes back to private companies.

It was an encounter Roosevelt would not soon forget.

And it would not be the last time he and Lindbergh would clash.

In the summer of 1933, Charles and Anne (acting as navigator and radio operator) took off on an ambitious transatlantic flight for Pan Am.

The trip was successful — probably the most important flight they had ever taken together. They accomplished their primary purpose, which was to check the bases and survey the air routes. They also used the flight to test new instruments. (One, invented by Lindbergh, was called a "sky hook." It gathered airborne bacteria on a slide covered with petroleum jelly.)

The 30,000-mile, five-and-a-half-month flight was an arduous undertaking. Lindbergh considered it more hazardous than his flight to Paris. They encountered blizzards, hurricanes, sandstorms, and nearly every type of extreme weather and hazardous flying condition.

> We flew along the North American coast to Labrador, spent several weeks surveying Greenland, landed in Iceland, the Faeroes, and the Shetlands en route to the continent of Europe, visited all Atlantic countries between Norway and Portugal, with side expeditions inland to Sweden, Finland, Russia, Holland and Switzerland.
>
> — Charles Lindbergh

For me, the trip was the nearest approximation to "a life of our own" that could then be found. It meant more freedom, more privacy with my husband, and more contact with people in natural surroundings. In addition, there was the satisfaction of taking a practical

part in the work of the expedition as radio operator and copilot-navigator. I carried my part in the project and shared the triumphs of successful accomplishment.
— Anne Morrow Lindbergh

During the five and a half months they were gone, Jon was left with his grandmother Evangeline and Betty Gow at the Morrows' summer home in Maine. There was some unfavorable public reaction to the trip. Some found it odd that the Lindberghs, who had just lost a son, would leave their second son alone for such a long time at such a young age. He celebrated his first birthday without his mother and father.

LEAVING

Charles believed that the guards, Thor, and other measures he was taking might protect his son from the lunatic letter writers and the would-be kidnappers. But the media, he was convinced, would never allow his family to lead a normal life.

He went so far as to issue an appeal:

Mrs. Lindbergh and I have made our home in New Jersey. It is natural that we should wish to continue to live there near our friends and interests. Obviously, however, it is impossible for us to subject the life of our second son to the publicity which we feel was in large measure responsible for the death of our first. We feel that our children have the right to grow up normally with other children. Continued publicity will make this impossible. I am appealing to the Press to permit our children to live the lives of normal Americans.

The appeal accomplished nothing.

And there were some terrifying moments. Twice while going to nursery school, Jon was frightened by photographers.

A final incident convinced us of the impossibility of giving our son a normal life in this country. The car that was carrying him home from school in Englewood was chased by [a carful of] newspaper photographers and forced to the curb, where one of the men jumped out and took photographs of the terrified child.

— Anne Morrow Lindbergh

Jon had to be taken out of nursery school. On the grounds of the Morrow estate, he played inside a wire mesh enclosure while shotgun-toting guards patrolled the area.

Charles had grown to loathe the media, but he blamed, in part, the American people themselves. Struggling to come to terms with her son's death, Anne was, at times, deeply depressed. Charles, always in complete control of his emotions, gave no indication of his mental state.

The dangers of fanatics, gangsters, and newspapermen made life close to intolerable for my wife and son, and in consequence for me. I considered moving to some other section of the United States, but concluded that we would gain little more security and peace. Press publicity would certainly follow wherever we went, and no state could give us greater assistance than we were receiving from New Jersey and its police. . . . I could not work efficiently . . . under the circumstances that existed, and I felt uncomfortable about making any trips away from home . . .

— Charles Lindbergh

Lindbergh concluded it was necessary to leave the United States.

My wife and I decided to go first to England, because we had been told that Englishmen respected rights of privacy and that English newspapers had more respect for law than ours at home. Kidnapping and gangsterism such as we had experienced in the United States were unknown in the British Isles. British policemen enforced the law unarmed. We knew the common language would be an advantage, and in England we had friends. Also, quite simply, we had been attracted by British tourist-bureau advertisements that described the beauties of the countryside and welcomed visitors.

— Charles Lindbergh

ENGLAND

On December 22, 1935, unknown to the American public, the Lindberghs boarded a freighter bound for Liverpool, England. Charles was reluctant to leave on a regular passenger ship. Even the crew of the freighter was unaware of their identities until they had set sail. He had even obtained their passports secretly. During the trip Anne and Jon ate together while Charles dined with the captain. Thor came over soon after.

In the United States, civic groups and newspapers spoke out about the meaning of America's most revered hero being forced to leave.

> [It is] unbelievable that conditions should make it impossible for people as valuable as the Lindberghs to live here.
>
> — The National Congress of Parents and Teachers

> The excesses of American habit and temperament are an old story. They have yielded prime virtues such as hospitality and generosity. But they have produced not less barbarism and cheapness and it is high time that the nation viewed these facts candidly, and accepted the truth about its faults. The slow, hard task of curbing the violence of its public moods cannot be too speedily begun.
>
> — The New York *Herald-Tribune*

Charles and Anne Morrow Lindbergh, with son Jon, arrive in Liverpool, England, December 1935.

These speeches and editorials asked what the departure of the Lindberghs from the country of their birth said about American society, and blamed the sensation-seeking tabloid papers for the situation.

Their friends soon helped the Lindberghs find a charming fourteenth-century house in the English countryside, not too far from London.

At first the British reporters were not much better than their American counterparts. But interest in the Lindberghs soon lagged and Charles and Anne began to enjoy the privacy they had hoped to find. For the first time since they had met they were able to walk and shop together.

Anne, who had been writing since her college years, loved the antique-filled house and enjoyed writing there. The year they left the United States, *North to the Orient,* her account of their 1931 Pacific flight, was published. It was well received by the critics and became a best-seller. (The book contained maps drawn by Charles.) While living in England she wrote *Listen, the Wind,* which was about their

The Lindberghs' country home, in Kent, England.

five-and-a-half-month transoceanic survey flight. It, too, was destined to become a critical and commercial success.

FRANCE

The Lindberghs spent two years in England before moving to a remote island off the coast of France. In part the move was made because Charles wanted to be closer to Dr. Carrel, the French scientist he had met in 1930.

The small island with its three-story stone house was found for them by Carrel and his wife, who were their only neighbors. At low tide they could walk to the larger island where the Carrels lived. There was no running water, electricity, or plumbing but the inconveniences were more than made up for by the solitude, which both Anne and Charles enjoyed. (Once, flying over the house, Charles dropped Anne a note telling her when he would be home for dinner.)

Carrel and Lindbergh continued their close working relationship and collaborated on a book. They discussed their progress in the laboratory, as well as other issues that concerned them both.

Lindbergh believed that learning to fly proved humans were capable of working miracles. He began to consider the possibility of extending life, perhaps indefinitely. He studied biology, cytology, organic chemistry, and surgery, and set up a laboratory at one end of the house. He constantly shared his ideas with Carrel, who had plenty of ideas of his own about humankind.

Carrel believed in the superiority of the white race, which he felt was being threatened by a rising tide of Asian and other "colored" races. He advocated exterminating criminals, the insane, and anyone else who, in Carrel's estimation, would weaken white civilization.

"There is no escaping the fact that men were definitely not created equal . . ." Carrel said in an interview.

He urged his fellow white men to do what was necessary to maintain white supremacy.

Lindbergh agreed with much of what Carrel was saying.

Both he and Anne had become interested in politics and the state of the world. Charles gave considerable thought to American politics. He found it corrupt and misdirected. He pondered whether to take an active role in pointing the country in the direction in which he believed it should be headed.

During his exchange with Roosevelt over the airmail issue, Lindbergh's friends had urged him to enter the political arena. Some (and many of his friends were in a position to know) assured him that the presidential nomination could be his. While Lindbergh weighed his choices, the world prepared to go to war.

Chapter Ten

THE WINDS OF WAR

. . . Hitler, I am beginning to feel, is like an inspired religious leader, and as such fanatical — a visionary who really wants the best for his country.
— Anne Morrow Lindbergh

No system of representation can succeed in which the voice of weakness is equal to the voice of strength.
— Charles Lindbergh

GERMANY

In the summer of 1936, Lindbergh was asked by the American military attaché in Berlin if he would be willing to inspect and report on the state of German military aviation.

In 1919, after Germany lost World War I, the victorious nations — England, France, and the United States — had imposed severe limitations on Germany's military and in-

189

dustrial growth. The country was virtually disarmed, tanks and planes severely restricted.

By 1936, however, after three years of rule by Adolf Hitler, Germany had rearmed, including building up its air force. The military attaché, fearing that American intelligence was inadequate, wanted Lindbergh's expert assessment. (The idea had been suggested to him by his wife, who had read about Lindbergh inspecting aviation facilities in France.)

In late July, once again leaving Jon in the care of others, the Lindberghs left for the German capital. They attended the opening ceremonies of the summer Olympics as the guests of Field Marshal Hermann Goering, who was the head of the Luftwaffe, the German air force, and the second most powerful man in Germany.

The Olympic games held in Berlin in August 1936 afforded the Nazis a golden opportunity to impress the world with the achievements of the Third Reich, and they made the most of it. The signs . . . (Jews Not Welcome) were quietly hauled down from the shops, hotels, beer gardens and places of public entertain-

Adolf Hitler.

Lindbergh in Germany with the American military attaché.

ment, the persecution of the Jews and of the two Christian churches temporarily halted, and the country put on its best behavior. . . . The visitors, especially those from England and America, were greatly impressed by what they saw: apparently a happy, healthy, friendly people united under Hitler — a far different picture, they said, than they had got from reading the newspaper dispatches from Berlin.

— William L. Shirer, journalist

Lindbergh was shown aircraft production facilities and airfields and was briefed by Nazi officials. They told him about Germany's plans to make the Luftwaffe the finest air force in the world.

Lindbergh reported that the Luftwaffe was already superior to the air forces of all the European countries combined. He was impressed by the number of factories, their production capabilities, and the strides the Germans had made in the past few years. The Luftwaffe was, according to Lindbergh, invincible.

I was deeply impressed by the number and efficiency of German factories and laboratories, but the unparalleled destructive power that the Luftwaffe was building alarmed me. I realized that in a few more years it would be possible for bombers to wipe out hundreds of thousands in the great cities of Europe. I had always thought of aviation as symbolizing the advance of civilization. Here, in an extremely disturbing contradiction, I saw aviation advancing the destruction of civilization . . . I knew theoretically what modern bombs could do to cities. At the same time, experiences in war games had convinced me that claims for the effectiveness of both ground and air defense were tremendously exaggerated. In Nazi Germany, for the first time, war became real to me. The officers I met were not preparing for a game. Their discussions gave me a sense of blood and bullets, and I realized how destructive my profession of aviation might become.

— Charles Lindbergh

His report was incorporated into that of the military attaché and sent to Washington, D.C.

But the accuracy of Lindbergh's report was questionable. He spoke no German and never interviewed a civilian or had any unofficial conversations. He was constantly accompanied by Nazi officials.

Goering had orchestrated the visit, flattering the Lindberghs, showing the aviator only what he wanted him to see and exaggerating Germany's actual strength and future capability. The Germans didn't have as many planes as Lindbergh thought, nor were their factories capable of producing the number of planes that Lindbergh reported. Goering hoped the respected aviation hero would convince other countries of Germany's overwhelming superiority. Lindbergh's report suggested that military opposition to Germany was futile.

Over the next two years (1937 and 1938) the Lindberghs returned twice to Nazi Germany. News photos showed them both smiling and enjoying themselves in public. The Lindberghs came to admire and respect what they perceived as the characteristics of Adolf Hitler's Nazi Germany.

The organized vitality of Germany was what most impressed me: the unceasing activity of the people, and the convinced dictatorial direction to create the new factories, airfields, and research laboratories. Militarism was pervasive — streets were full of uniforms and banners.

— Charles Lindbergh

First impressions driving in: the newness of things, streets, buildings, houses. The neatness, order, trimness, cleanliness . . . The activity, lots of people on streets . . . nice clothes . . . no sense of poverty. Lots of bicycles and cars. The sense of festivity, flags hung out, the Nazi flag, red with a swastika on it, *everywhere* . . . Avenues hung with flags, islands of tall standards, flags of the world. Lots of building going up along roads.

— Anne Morrow Lindbergh

. . . There is no question of the power, unity and purposefulness of Germany. It is terrific. I have never in my life been so conscious of such a *directed* force. It is thrilling when seen manifested in the energy, pride, and morale of the people — especially the young people.

— Anne Morrow Lindbergh

The new Germany seemed ambitious, alive, organized, clean, and purposeful. The Lindberghs enjoyed being surrounded by the militaristic atmosphere — the flags flying and the streets filled with soldiers.

Flags hide the buildings and line the streets. Sounds of bands in distance; looking down closed streets, you can see boys or young men massing, with flags. A public building with a balcony draped for a speech. All kinds

Hitler tours triumphantly as he promises to build a stronger nation.

of uniforms in the streets . . . Hitler's special shock troops . . . boy scouts and . . . girl scouts. The boys wear black corduroy shorts and brown shirts. The girls wear quite long black skirts. (Hitler likes modesty in women!) The crowds are awe-struck. "*Wunderbar!*" It is a great show.

— Anne Morrow Lindbergh

THE MEDAL

In October 1938, Lindbergh was the guest of honor at a dinner given by the United States ambassador to Germany. Goering presented Lindbergh with the Service Cross of the German Eagle — Germany's second highest decoration.

Göring was the last to arrive. I was standing at the back of the room when he came through the door, wearing a blue Luftwaffe uniform of new design. He seemed less stout than when I last saw him. Heads turned and conversation dropped . . . I noticed that Göring carried a red box and some papers in one hand. When he came to me he handed me the box and papers and spoke several sentences in German. I knew no German but I soon learned that he had presented me with the Order of the German Eagle, one of the highest decorations of the government — "by order of der Fuhrer," he said.

— Charles Lindbergh

Lindbergh wore the medal hung from a red ribbon around his neck for the remainder of the evening, mingling with high-ranking Nazi officers in attendance.

Less than a month later, *Kristallnacht*, the night of broken glass, occurred. At the time, *Kristallnacht* appeared to be a spontaneous riot by Germans angered at the Jewish population. Two days earlier, on November 7, 1938, a seventeen-year-old Polish Jewish boy whose family resided in Germany had shot a Nazi official at the German embassy in Paris. The boy's father, along with thousands of other Polish Jews, had been forcibly expelled from Germany and deported to Poland. All their possessions had to be left behind, and they were taken in trains and trucks in bitterly cold weather. Grief stricken, the boy had been planning to avenge his father's persecution by shooting the German ambassador to France, but in his rage shot the lower-ranking official.

But the rioting that began on the night of November 9, when the officer died of his wounds, was not spontaneous. The rising anger against the Jews was systematically fueled by the Nazi propaganda machine. The rioting was sanctioned by the government (the police were told not to in-

The Lindberghs with Goering at his home in Berlin.

trude) and directed and executed by the Nazi military police.

Thousands of buildings belonging to Jews — synagogues, businesses, and homes — were set on fire all over Germany. The plateglass windows of Jewish businesses were smashed, hence the name *Kristallnacht*. Thousands of Jewish citizens were beaten, including women and children, and between 20,000 and 30,000 Jews were arrested and sent to concentration camps.

Kristallnacht was the worst outbreak of violence against the Jewish population in Germany up to that time. Now the Nazis' brutal policy regarding the Jews was no longer the subject of speculation. Following *Kristallnacht* the Nazis instituted new, repressive, anti-Semitic laws. Jews were not allowed to be managers or executives involved in business, and were not permitted to sell their wares or services. Jewish children were not allowed to attend school, and curfews were imposed. Jews were forbidden to go to the movies, theaters, or to eat in restaurants; they were prohibited from beaches and resorts.

In the United States, *Kristallnacht* shocked portions of the American public and opened many eyes to the brutality and the violence that had come to characterize the Nazi government.

The Lindberghs' visits to Germany — visits they clearly enjoyed, where they were wined and dined by the same people who were having unarmed men and women gunned down in the streets — were seen by many as, to say the least, inappropriate.

Many Americans began to question Lindbergh's judgment and his politics. He was faulted for accepting the medal and refusing to return it once having seen the furor it caused. Movie audiences in the United States hissed when he appeared in newsreels.

Lindbergh saw no reason to return the medal. Diplomatic relations between the United States and Germany were normal at that time. The medal was no different to him from the dozens of others he had received. He had no intention of returning it.

MUNICH

Munich, Germany, was the site of a momentous meeting between Hitler and the prime ministers of England and France. Neville Chamberlain, England's prime minister, was inclined to go as far as he could in acquiescing to Hitler's demands for more land for the German people. Chamberlain believed that this was the best course to preserve peace in Europe.

At their Munich meeting, Chamberlain and Hitler signed a pact agreeing that they would never again go to war against each other. This meant that England would do nothing while Germany took a large part of Czechoslovakia. Chamberlain hoped this would satisfy Hitler, who assured him it would. Chamberlain returned to cheering crowds in England, announcing "I believe it is peace in our time." He was tragically mistaken.

On October 1, 1938, German troops crossed into Czechoslovakia.

Chamberlain's fatally flawed decision to appease Hitler was based, in large part, on his fear of German military strength. The fear may have been made worse by the fact that Chamberlain had read Lindbergh's report on the Luftwaffe shortly before leaving for Munich:

Chamberlain upon his return from Munich, holding the Munich pact.

I am by no means convinced that England and France could win a war against Germany at the present time, but, whether they win or lose, all of the participating countries would probably be prostrated by their efforts . . . I am convinced that it is wiser to permit Germany's eastward expansion than to throw England and France, unprepared, into a war at this time.

We must recognize the fact that the Germans are a great and able people. Their military strength now makes them inseparable from the welfare of European civilization, for they have the power either to preserve or destroy it. For the first time in history, a nation has the power either to save or ruin the great cities of Europe. Germany has such a preponderance of war planes that she can bomb any city in Europe with comparatively little resistance. England and France are too weak in the air to protect themselves.

— Charles Lindbergh

THE WAVE OF THE FUTURE

Lindbergh was impressed by the Nazis. They had once again turned Germany, only recently the weakest country in Europe, into a modern military power. Hitler had accomplished a great deal in a short period of time. Some of his politics, Lindbergh grudgingly admitted, were, perhaps, a bit excessive but he felt Hitler's extraordinary accomplishments would overshadow his shortcomings. He scoffed at those who considered Hitler a madman who was about to engulf the world in war. Lindbergh considered Hitler much too sane for that.

He cautioned that were war to break out, Germany would win, but there would really be no winners — victors and vanquished would emerge from the rubble greatly weakened. This would allow the Russian Communists — who, according to Lindbergh, were the real enemies — to take over Europe.

He recommended that Britain and France support Germany's industrial and military growth. Lindbergh believed that a strong Germany meant a strong Europe and the continued survival of white, European civilization.

He and Anne believed that the new Fascist German state was "the wave of the future." Anne wrote a book by that name, which explained that there were some rough edges to the Nazi philosophy but:

> . . . is some new, and perhaps even ultimately good, conception of humanity trying to come to birth . . . ? The wave of the future is coming and there is no fighting it.
>
> — Anne Morrow Lindbergh

The book was published in 1940 and the reaction to it was unfavorable.

The Lindberghs liked Nazi Germany so much that in the winter of 1938 they considered moving their family (including their third son, Land, who was born May 12, 1937) to Berlin. But as the world moved closer to war, they reconsidered and returned to the shores of the United States.

Chapter Eleven

$\mathcal{F}$ALL FROM $\mathcal{G}$RACE

*Knowing the United States would be put under high
pressure to enter the war, I laid plans to take an active part
in opposing this step.*

— Charles Lindbergh

THE ISOLATIONISTS

After returning to the United States in April 1939, Lindbergh resigned his commission in the military so he could
speak out freely, as a civilian, against American involvement
in the war.

... I decided to return to America, risking, possibly,
gangsterism, and despite publicity and the problems
involved in bringing my family home ... I saw no further contribution I could make to improve the rela-

tionships between European countries. If there was to be a war, then my place was back in my own country. I felt I could exercise a constructive influence in America by warning people of the danger of the Soviet Union and by explaining that the destruction of Hitler, even if it could be accomplished through using American resources, would probably result in enhancing the still-greater menace of Stalin. I would argue for an American policy of strength and neutrality, one that would encourage European nations to take the responsibility for their own relationships and destinies.

— Charles Lindbergh

In September, just two weeks after England and France had declared war on Germany, Lindbergh gave his first nationwide radio address. Although not as popular as he had been before accepting the German medal, Lindbergh was still popular enough to attract a huge listening audience — an audience as large as that which tuned in to President Roosevelt's eagerly awaited "fireside chats."

. . . I knew prowar forces were powerful, with President Roosevelt the strongest and most subtle of their leaders. I had concluded that he was lacking in a statesman's wisdom, but I did not doubt that he was one of the cleverest politicians ever born. Regardless of the fact that he had publicly advocated a policy of neutrality for the United States, it seemed to me apparent that he intended to lead our country into the war. The powers he influenced and controlled were great. Opposing them would require planning, political skill,

and organization. For me, this meant entertaining a
new framework of life.

— Charles Lindbergh

Lindbergh chose to broadcast the speech from Washington, D.C., rather than New York City, even though it was
closer to his Long Island home. The Lindberghs had continued to receive threatening letters since the days of the
kidnapping. Lindbergh hoped that by broadcasting from
Washington he would be able to spare his family any more
attention. He knew his views could cause more difficulties
but he felt compelled to speak out.

According to Lindbergh, Roosevelt, through intermedi-
aries, pressured him to cancel the address. They offered, he
said, the to-be-created cabinet post of secretary of a separate
Department of the Air Force. The position would be his if
he would take out those parts of the speech that criticized
administration policy or agree not to give the speech at all.

Roosevelt, who remembered Lindbergh well from their
confrontation over the airmail contracts six years earlier,
considered him a potentially powerful foe. Privately he
voiced darker views: "If I should die tomorrow, I want you
to know this. I am absolutely convinced that Lindbergh is a
Nazi."

Lindbergh's voice was well suited to America's newest
mass medium. He addressed himself to Americans who believed, as he did, that the country was not at risk due to the
conflict in Europe — that the war in Europe was more like
a family feud and it was best the United States remained on
the sidelines.

The speech was front-page news and generated a great

deal of comment. Most critical were members of the Roosevelt administration.

In the next eighteen months Lindbergh delivered five radio broadcasts, addressed meetings, appeared at rallies, wrote articles, and testified before congressional committees.

> Various prowar and antiwar groups became active in the ensuing months. My own role as I spoke, wrote, and took action was as an independent citizen, co-operating with antiwar groups, meeting with Congressmen and Senators, testifying before committees, writing articles, making addresses. Every poll taken showed a large majority of the American populace to be against participation in the war. Yet it was obvious that the United States was moving constantly closer to belligerency.
>
> — Charles Lindbergh

He opposed giving aid of any kind to England. He explained that any aid given would be wasted, because the Germans were invincible. The best way for the United States to protect herself would be to prepare her defenses at home, to protect the continent in the unlikely event that the protective expanse of the Atlantic Ocean could be bridged by an invading army. Lindbergh had become one of the leading spokesmen for the isolationist philosophy.

At the time many Americans agreed with Lindbergh. Although they might have been sympathetic to the plight of England, the majority of the population was against sending arms, and even more opposed to America's entry into the war.

But by late 1940, opinion had begun to change. That summer the German army had overrun Belgium, Norway, the Netherlands, Luxembourg, and, in June, France. England was left to fight on alone. Many began to wonder whether the war would remain a "family feud." They began to question the wisdom of the isolationist philosophy, a philosophy that Lindbergh had come to symbolize.

He is a blind young man if he really believes we can live on terms of equal peace and happiness "regardless of which side wins this war" in Europe. Colonel Lindbergh remains a great flyer.

— *The New York Times*

THE BATTLE OF BRITAIN

England's valiant lone struggle further served to sway the American public. In late May and early June 1940, 340,000 British and French soldiers, seemingly trapped at Dunkirk, a seaport on the coast of France, were miraculously evacuated:

A fleet of nearly nine-hundred widely varied craft — speedboats, yachts, Channel ferries, tugs with strings of barges attached, lifeboats, passenger ships, naval vessels; all save the naval ships were manned by civilian volunteers — crisscrossed the Channel, often under attack from the air, to pluck from Dunkirk's harbor and beaches and carry off to English ports . . . the whole of the [British Expeditionary Force] save those who had to fight to the last to cover the withdrawal . . . 338,226 troops had been borne to England

by June 4 . . . The operation would not have been possible without temporary domination of the local sky
by the [British] Royal Air Force which, battling
against great numerical odds, had decisively defeated
the Luftwaffe: Hurricanes and Spitfires had knocked
down three or four German bombers and fighters for
every plane lost of their own.

Americans began to believe that England's chances might
be better than people such as Lindbergh thought.

The Royal Air Force (RAF) also played a key role in the
Battle of Britain, which began in August 1940, when the
Luftwaffe launched daily air attacks over England. British
children were evacuated from the island nation's targeted
cities to the safety of the small towns and farms in the countryside. Frightened and confused, carrying toothbrushes,
towels, and gas masks, they were placed on buses by concerned parents, teachers, and social workers.

The Luftwaffe was able to inflict devastating damage on
England's cities, especially London. It was never able, however, to gain control of the skies over England, control denied by the RAF. The German air force had been built
to lend tactical air support to ground operations: Hitler's
"Blitzkreig" or lightning war. However, it lacked the fighters that were needed to gain air superiority and the long-
range heavy bombers necessary in the Battle of Britain.

Denied air superiority, the Germans were unable to launch
a full-scale land invasion of England as they had hoped.

The determined, inspirational eloquence of Prime Minister Winston Churchill also began to have an effect on people in the United States:

We shall go on to the end, we shall fight in France, we shall fight in the seas and oceans, we shall fight with growing confidence and growing strength in the air, we shall defend our island, whatever the cost may be, we shall fight on the beaches, we shall fight on the landing-grounds, we shall fight in the fields and in the streets, we shall fight in the hills; we shall never surrender, and even if, which I do not for a moment believe, this island or a large part of it were subjugated and starving, then our Empire beyond the seas, armed and guarded by the British Fleet, would carry on the struggle until, in God's good time, the New World, with all its power and might, steps forth to the rescue and liberation of the Old.

— Winston Churchill

Winston Churchill. The "V for victory" sign he makes here symbolizes the confidence he tried to instill in the British people to stave off the German offensive.

Despite Lindbergh's prediction that England would surely be defeated by Germany, the British held on, while American public opinion and events pulled the United States closer to war.

"LEND-LEASE"

By early 1941, Roosevelt was calling for the United States to become the "Arsenal of Democracy." The President wanted to provide England with the war material needed in order to continue to fight the Germans. The policy that had most recently prevailed was the so-called cash-and-carry provision of the 1935 Neutrality Law.

Cash-and-carry meant that England would have to pay for and transport these goods at the time of purchase. England, nearly out of money, would be unable to do this. Roosevelt proposed "lend-lease" in order to ease the burdens of cash-and-carry.

Lend-lease, Roosevelt explained simply and brilliantly, was the neighborly thing to do:

> Suppose my neighbor's home catches fire and I have got a length of garden hose four or five hundred feet away; but, my heaven, if he can take my garden hose and connect it up with his hydrant, I may help him put out his fire . . . I don't say to him before that operation, "Neighbor, my garden hose cost me $15; you have got to pay me $15 for it." I don't want $15 — I want my garden hose back after the fire is over.

Congress, accurately reflecting public opinion, passed the Lend-Lease Act by a wide margin.

By the end of 1941, Americans in greater numbers were coming to believe that England's fate was their fate, and that Hitler's ideas represented an evil that had to be opposed by force. They believed that despite the protective moat of the Atlantic Ocean, Germany and her allies, Italy and Japan, did in fact pose a direct threat to the United States. Americans began to feel that the United States should, short of entering the war, aid England in any way it could.

Many Americans, however, continued to believe in the isolationist philosophy.

AMERICA FIRST

The most powerful isolationist group in the United States was the America First Committee (AFC). The AFC was founded in September 1940, and at its peak had an estimated 850,000 members. Many prominent Americans — politicians, movie stars, writers, and business leaders — joined pacifists, isolationists, and American Nazis to compose the membership of America First.

Following his successful nationwide radio address, the AFC leadership approached Lindbergh and asked him to become a speaker for the organization. Lindbergh agreed and also joined the AFC's executive committee. He made it clear that he would not accept any money for speaking, would pay his own expenses, and would not submit his speeches for approval.

On April 17, 1941, Lindbergh delivered his first major address as a member of the AFC. He restated many of the ideas he had spoken about over the past three years, including his belief that England's defeat by Germany was inevitable.

France has now been defeated and, despite the propaganda and confusion of recent months, it is now obvious that England is losing the war. I believe this is realized even by the British Government. But they have one last desperate plan remaining. They hope they may be able to persuade us to send...American... Force(s) to Europe.

— Charles Lindbergh

Lindbergh appealed to those Americans who believed that the United States had been tricked into entering World

The America First rally in Madison Square Garden, October 30, 1941, where Lindbergh spoke to 20,000 people.

War I by politicians and businessmen interested in personal financial gain and not the lofty ideals they spoke of — such as making the world safe for democracy. He spoke in Chicago, New York's Madison Square Garden, the Hollywood Bowl and, in fact, in every state in the country. He became the most popular, powerful, and prestigious spokesman for the isolationist movement. And he was soon to become its most controversial.

DES MOINES

Few Americans have been so lavishly praised as Charles A. Lindbergh; few have been so severely denounced as he, for his opposition to American entry into World War II. Some simply criticized his foreign policy analyses and found them mistaken or unwise. Many questioned his qualifications to speak on foreign affairs. But, increasingly, especially in 1941, critics challenged his loyalty, his patriotism, and his dedication to democracy. In the eyes of millions of Americans then and later he was seen as little better than a Nazi.

— Wayne S. Cole, historian

On September 11, 1941, speaking in Des Moines, Iowa, Lindbergh delivered his most pointed attack yet on those he claimed were pushing the United States toward war for selfish reasons. For months he had been talking about these pressure groups. Now he decided to name them.

The three most important groups who have been pressing this country toward war are the British, the

Lindbergh's speeches were impassioned and controversial. Despite his desire for privacy, he made frequent public appearances for the AFC.

Jewish and the Roosevelt Administration . . . I believe
I have named the major war agitators in this country.

Months before the speech Lindbergh had outlined his
thoughts on the subject in his diary:

The pressure for war is high and mounting. The people are opposed to it, but the Administration seems to
have "the bit in its teeth" and hell-bent on its way to
war. Most of the Jewish interests in the country are behind war, and they control a huge part of our press and
radio and most of our motion pictures.

His speech continued, concluding with a vague threat:

But no person of honesty and vision can look on their
prowar policy here today without seeing the dangers in
that policy, both for us and for them. Instead of agitat-
ing for war, the Jewish groups in this country should
be opposing it in every possible way, for they will be
among the first to feel its consequences.

Lindbergh did not clarify the threat any further. But to
many, the implications were clear: If the Jews didn't cease
their lobbying they would pay.

To many Americans — politicians, journalists, religious
leaders, and citizens — Charles Lindbergh no longer
sounded like someone who sincerely believed it was wrong
for America to become involved in the war. He sounded
more like someone who simply disliked Jews.

Others, although deeply troubled by his apparent anti-

Semitism, felt it was more important to question his qualifications. Why should someone speak on American foreign
policy simply because he had flown a plane over the ocean?
Others went further and questioned his patriotism, and
called the speech un-American. In fact, the FBI had opened
a file on Lindbergh in the fall of 1939.

Some members of the America First Committee,
shocked by the content and tone of the speech, resigned in
protest. Others remained as members but refused to speak
in public for fear of being associated with Lindbergh's anti-
Semitic views.

Many Americans who shared Lindbergh's isolationist
views urged him to speak out about the brutalities and cru-
elties that the Nazis were inflicting on thousands of unarmed men, women, and children — a government policy
that would eventually result in the killing of ten million
people. But, other than a brief mention of Nazi persecution
of the Jews in the Des Moines speech, Lindbergh refused to
utter a word about it in public.

Civic organizations repudiated their association with
him. Lindbergh's name no longer appeared on the water
tower in his hometown. Friends, business associates, and
relatives severed their ties with him. Harry Breckenridge,
his long-time lawyer, and Harry Guggenheim, one of his
first patrons, would have nothing to do with him. Anne's
mother and sister publicly opposed him. Anne, on the other
hand, not only supported her husband but agreed with
him — as she made clear in her book, *The Wave of the Future*. She appeared with him on the speaker's platform when
he was giving a speech (although she did not join the
America First Committee).

DAY OF INFAMY

At 7:55 A.M., on Sunday, December 7, 1941, two waves of Japanese bombers attacked the U.S. naval base at Pearl Harbor, Hawaii. Over fourteen ships and 188 airplanes were lost. Two thousand four hundred Americans were killed and another 1,000 injured. It was the worst naval defeat in American history.

On December 8, the Senate (unanimously) and the House (388 to 1) approved a declaration of war against Japan. Within days, Germany and Italy declared war on the United States. The world was at war.

The America First Committee disbanded immediately after the surprise attack on Pearl Harbor. Its members were

A fireball from the bombing of Pearl Harbor rises up from the wreckage as sailors at the Naval Air Station on Ford Island look on in disbelief.

urged to cease all opposition to the war and stand behind the president.

Lindbergh, who had resigned his military commission in 1939, wanted to serve in the military now that the nation was at war. Members of the Roosevelt administration, however, made it clear that he would have to admit his views had been wrong before his commission would be reinstated. Characteristically and predictably, Lindbergh refused.

Roosevelt apparently also took steps to thwart Lindbergh's attempt to work in the private sector. Pan Am, Curtiss-Wright, and United Aircraft all had been interested in employing Lindbergh. The offers, however, never materialized, perhaps due to pressure from the government.

Determined as always, Lindbergh set about helping his country's war effort. In April 1942, Lindbergh became a consultant to Henry Ford. The car manufacturer was mass-producing B-24 bombers in his Willow Run, Michigan, plant. Lindbergh, in 1927, had given Ford his first airplane ride. Ford and Lindbergh were kindred spirits. Ford had been a member of the AFC's executive board and was a well-known anti-Semite, who greatly admired Hitler and displayed his picture on his wall.

Lindbergh was not satisfied with the quality of construction on the B-24s and balked at the red tape and uninformed advice from various generals. There was little he could do about it, however. The necessity to build up America's war machine placed a priority on speed. Lindbergh's experience and skill played an important part in solving Willow Run's many production problems.

A year later, with pressure from the administration apparently eased, the United Aircraft Corporation hired Lindbergh as a consultant. United Aircraft was building single-engine fighter planes. But Lindbergh was unhappy — he wanted to fly. He had been training hard to stay in shape. He had even taken a course that would allow him to update his license to fly multiengined planes. The forty-one-year-old Lindbergh was in top physical condition. (Six years earlier he had held his breath for a record-making three minutes.)

Designated a civilian observer, Lindbergh flew dozens of combat missions as a test pilot in the Pacific theater, flying Lockheed P-30 "Lightnings," in the spring of 1944. This was, of course, strictly against the rules, but it was over-looked by Lindbergh's superiors, who still considered the "Lone Eagle" a hero.

He more than justified their faith in him. He displayed the skill and extraordinary physical attributes that had made him the world's most famous flyer. At one point, in competition with two of the Marine Corps' top pilots, he bested both in high altitude competition, out-gunning and out-flying them. The younger pilots, some half his age, were impressed with his instinctive abilities, courage, and knowledge.

Ground crews noticed that Lindbergh frequently re-turned from missions with more fuel remaining in his tank than his comrades. Lindbergh was able to do this because of the methods that he had learned when he was a barnstorm-ing pilot twenty years earlier. These "tricks of the trade" — not included in World War II training manuals — were unknown to the younger pilots. Lindbergh began giving talks on his methods.

During one mission, aimed at a Japanese oil installation, Lindbergh engaged in a head-on fight with an enemy plane:

I watched the red balls of the rising sun on the enemy plane grow larger, shrink from round to oval, then disappear as the wings cut toward me, knife-edged against the background of gray haze. It was to be a head-on pass. I centered the plane in my right sight and squeezed finger against trigger. Streaks of fire leapt from my fighter's nose out of four machine guns and one cannon. Raise the tracers — creep them leftward — flashes on the target as my bullets hit — but the wingspan widened in my ring sight. The enemy's guns were firing too. I held the trigger down, head on with no deflection. There was a rattle of machine guns and streams of tracers. Slightly climbing, slightly diving at five hundred miles an hour we approached, hurdling in an eternity of time and space . . . I hauled back on my stick as I sensed our closeness. The Japanese plane jerked upward, too! Was the pilot trying to collide? I yanked back with all my strength, braced for the crash. There was a bump but it was only air.

By how much did we miss? Ten feet? Five? I was zooming steeply. I banked left and saw ack-ack bursts ahead, reversed the bank and swept my eyes over sky and earth looking for aircraft. I saw only friendly Lightnings. No one but my wingman was on my tail. I saw the plane I had just shot down. My enemy was in a wingover, out of control. I watched his nose drop. His plane twisted as it gathered speed. The rising suns diminished in size. Down. Down. Down. The sea had not seemed so far beneath us. Down. A fountain of spray, white foam on water; ripples circled outward, merged with waves. The foam subsided. No mark remained.

— Charles Lindbergh

America's entry into World War II, coupled with England's heroic efforts and the Russians forcing Hitler to fight a war on two fronts, eventually turned the tide of the war. On June 6, 1944, D-Day, the Allied forces landed on the coast of France. In August 1944, Paris was liberated, and on May 8, 1945, the war in Europe was over.

On August 6, 1945, the United States dropped an atomic bomb on the Japanese city of Hiroshima. Three days later a second atomic bomb was dropped on the city of Nagasaki. Two hundred thousand people are estimated to have died as a result of these two attacks. A week later the Japanese surrendered, and the war was over.

For Lindbergh, the eighteen years of hero worship that he had so disliked were also over. He was an American hero no more.

> In promoting appeasement and military unpreparedness, Lindbergh damaged his country to a greater degree than any other private citizen in modern times. That he meant well makes no difference . . .
> — William O'Neill, historian

Chapter Twelve

*A*FTER THE *W*AR

After my death, the molecules of my being will return to the earth and the sky. They came from the stars. I am of the stars.
— Charles Lindbergh

THE CONSULTANT

Forty-eight-year-old Charles Lindbergh had never had a conventional nine-to-five job. He preferred, it seems, the less restrictive role of consultant. He became a technical consultant for the United States Air Force and Pan American Airways, advising them in a variety of areas, including testing new jets for the Air Force. His travel responsibilities took him around the world many times over, mostly traveling coach, under an assumed name, carrying only what would fit in the overhead luggage area. He was away from home for months at a time, and his Air Force duties often

223

meant his itinerary was confidential, kept secret even from his family.

THE AUTHOR

On and off for the previous twenty years, Lindbergh had worked on a book that combined the story of his 1927 flight with the story of his boyhood.

The Spirit of St. Louis was published in 1953 and was a critical as well as popular success. The best-selling book was a Main Selection of the Book-of-the-Month Club, was serialized in the *Saturday Evening Post* (which paid $100,000 for the rights), and won the Pulitzer prize for biography.

Reviewers praised not only Lindergh's storytelling ability but also his accomplished writing style. In fact, some speculated that Anne had written it. *The Spirit of St. Louis* was a financial success as well, earning the author a million dollars.

Warner Brothers reportedly paid a million dollars for the movie rights. Three years later, in 1957, the big-budget film (starring James Stewart, one of the biggest stars of the day) turned out to be a box-office disappointment. The younger members of the movie-going audience didn't know who Lindbergh was, and the older ones, remembering all too well his pro-German ideas, stayed away.

Anne's literary reputation was enhanced when *Gift From the Sea* was published in 1956. It was on the best-seller lists for almost a year and was to become one of the best-selling books of the decade. Anne Morrow Lindbergh had become one of the most popular writers in America, especially among women, who admired her thoughts on the role of women in modern society.

THE FATHER

> You know Charles, he'll be here when he's here.
> — Anne Morrow Lindbergh

Since the kidnapping, the Lindberghs had lived in a succession of rented homes. In 1946, they had bought a big house on three wooded acres near Darien, Connecticut. The house on Long Island Sound was the first real home the children had known. There were nine bedrooms — one for each of the five children (Jon, Land, Anne Spencer who was born in 1940, Scott who was born in 1942, and Reeve who was born in 1945) — and six-and-a-half baths, as well as a study for Charles, Anne, and their secretary.

Thanks to his diminished popularity, the media began to leave the Lindberghs alone. And to a degree, this meant that the lives of the Lindbergh family were more normal than ever before. They took long walks together, played games, went on picnics, swam in the Sound, and had discussions

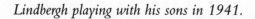

Lindbergh playing with his sons in 1941.

about books and other topics of interest. They did not, however, talk about the kidnapping or their father's World War II activities. The children found out about both on their own and by accident. (Charles and Anne, in fact, never talked about the kidnapping to each other.)

Anne Spencer learned about the kidnapping when someone came to the door claiming to be Charles, Jr. (People claiming to be the Lindberghs' first-born son were an all-too-frequent occurrence. The local police kept a close watch on the situation.) Scott learned about the kidnapping from a book in the library. Reeve didn't hear about her father's World War II philosophy until she was a freshman in college.

"Father," as he liked to be called, tried to teach his children the values *his* father had taught him: independence, honesty, fearlessness, and confidence. He also taught them how to climb trees, use tools, shoot guns, and swim (Jon learned via the "sink or swim" method by which Charles was taught — being thrown into the deep end of a pool). Charles enjoyed playing and competing with his children, but refused to lose any games on purpose.

When he was home, which was not often, the children made sure they behaved. "Father" demanded respect and was not above spanking the children if he felt the situation warranted it. Most of the time, however, he was off on one of his frequent and lengthy trips. Then they acted more like kids. Anne, with the help of nursemaids, cooks, housekeepers, and secretaries, was responsible for running the house. Charles rarely called or wrote and, at times, they didn't even know where he was.

Charles had wanted more children, perhaps as many as twelve, but Anne refused.

In the early 1960s, with the children growing up and leaving for college, marriage, and traveling in Europe, the Lindberghs sold the big house and moved into a smaller one on the property. They also had a chalet in Switzerland and a cottage on Maui where they began to spend their winters.

THE HERO

In 1962, John F. Kennedy and his wife, Jacqueline, invited the Lindberghs to a State dinner at the White House. The Kennedys were at the social pinnacle of the early 1960s, and the invitation marked the beginning of Lindbergh's reemergence as an American hero. When Kennedy's father, Joe, was the American ambassador to England during the prewar years, he had agreed strongly with Lindbergh's views. They shared a disdain for the British and an admiration for the Germans. By inviting Lindbergh to the White House, Kennedy bestowed his stamp of approval, which did much to give new luster to the Lone Eagle's tarnished image.

Lyndon Johnson, who succeeded Kennedy when he was assassinated in November 1963, continued the resurrection by inviting the Lindberghs to a number of official occasions, including a 1968 State dinner with the *Apollo 8* astronauts, who were about to take off for their historic moon-orbiting mission.

Lindbergh told the astronauts about his meetings with the father of rocketry, Robert Goddard, and about Goddard's visionary belief, nearly forty years earlier, in the possibilities of going to the moon. Of course Lindbergh, who had had the foresight to champion Goddard at a time when no one else did, had also seen the possibilities of space travel well before most. (Goddard, unrecognized in his lifetime, had died in 1945.) Lindbergh posed for a Polaroid shot, which one of the astronauts took with him into space.

In 1970, Lindbergh published his wartime journals, in which he continued to maintain the correctness of his views. He made no effort to modify, qualify, or apologize for those views — despite the evidence of the Nazi Holocaust. A *New York Times* review of the journal accurately reflected history's judgment:

> We do not believe that time has made Mr. Lindbergh's ideas more valid or that future historians will find them more persuasive than his contemporaries did. Like many civilized people in this country and abroad, he could not comprehend the radical evil of Nazism. Even in the retrospect of a quarter century he is unable to grasp it.

THE CONSERVATIONIST

> Where civilization is most advanced, few birds exist. I realize that if I would have to choose, I would rather have birds than airplanes.
>
> — Charles Lindbergh

Flying gave Lindbergh a bird's-eye view of the growing ecological tragedy that was threatening the future of the planet. By the early 1960s, Lindbergh had joined a growing number of people who were concerned about the effects of modern technology on the environment.

Lindbergh saw the damage all too clearly: the disappear-

Lindbergh in 1973.

ing forests, the polluted rivers and lakes, the deteriorating
atmosphere, and the species driven to the edge of extinc-
tion. He had grown up appreciating nature and animals
during his boyhood in rural Minnesota. Now he spent a
great deal of time reflecting on the course of modern civilization and the consequences of what was called "progress."

He decided that once again he had to take a public stand
on an issue that was vitally important. He joined the World
Wildlife Foundation as well as other conservation organizations. He began to put all his energy and time into the
conservation and ecology movement. He attended international conferences where he worked to protect endangered
species. He participated in fund-raising activities — speaking in public for the first time since World War II and giving a newspaper interview for the first time since the
kidnapping.

In late 1972, Lindbergh was forced to curtail his activities because of his health. After a series of illnesses — fevers, rashes, and severe weight loss — he was diagnosed as having an advanced case of lymphatic cancer. The doctors said he did not have long to live.

He was flown on a stretcher to his cottage on Maui, which had become his favorite residence. He planned his funeral as meticulously and calmly as he had planned his historic flight, forty-five years earlier. A Native-American poem would be read, hymns would be sung in Hawaiian, and he would be placed in an Hawaiian burial vault.

On August 25, 1974, the seventy-two-year-old Charles Lindbergh fell into a coma and died the next morning.

Lindbergh's gravestone with an inscription from the 139th Psalm: "If I take the wings of the morning, and dwell in the uttermost parts of the sea . . ."

*Anne Morrow Lindbergh in 1985 with a statue of her husband,
depicting him as both a young boy and a heroic aviator.*

SOURCE NOTES

PART ONE

p. 1   He is and . . .   William L. O'Neill, *A Democracy at War: America's Fight at Home and Abroad in World War II* (New York: The Free Press, 1993), p. 47.

Chapter One

p. 3   Life's values . . .   Charles A. Lindbergh, *Autobiography of Values* (San Diego: Harcourt Brace Jovanovich, 1978), p. 3.

p. 5   I hold . . .   Charles A. Lindbergh, *The Spirit of St. Louis* (New York: Charles Scribner's Sons, 1953), p. 373.

p. 9   I was . . .   Ibid, p. 376.

p. 10   With week-apart . . .   Leonard Mosley, *Lindbergh: A Biography* (Garden City, NY: Doubleday & Company, Inc., 1976), p. 10.

Chapter Two

p. 19   When I . . .   Ibid, p. 244.

p. 20   I cannot . . .   Russell Freedman, *The Wright Brothers: How They Invented the Airplane* (New York: Holiday House, 1991), p. 110.

p. 22   The roar . . .   Lindbergh, *The Spirit of St. Louis*, p. 250.

p. 26   At infrequent . . .   Ibid, p. 261.

p. 27   Life changed . . .   Ibid, p. 261.

p. 28   . . . I've never . . .   Ibid, p. 261.

p. 33   . . . (At) the Army . . .   Ibid, p. 405.

Chapter Three

p. 39   I had been . . .   Lindbergh, *Autobiography of Values*, p. 310.

p. 39   . . . I envisioned . . .   Ibid, p. 11.

p. 40   Why shouldn't . . .   Lindbergh, *The Spirit of St. Louis*, p. 15.

p. 41   St. Louis . . .   Ibid, p. 23.

p. 44   ... I'm not ...   Ibid, p. 26.
p. 45   ... I'm staring ...   Ibid, p. 74.
p. 46   "I'm afraid ..."   Ibid, p. 75.
p. 48   "It's going ..."   Ibid, p. 83, 84.
p. 49   "But then ..."   Ibid, p. 87.

Chapter Four

p. 55   The danger ...   Joshua Stoff, *Charles A. Lindbergh: A Photographic Album* (New York: Dover Publications, Inc. 1995), p. v.
p. 55   Almost as ...   Lindbergh, *The Spirit of St. Louis*, p. 150.
p. 57   He knew ...   Walter S. Ross, *The Last Hero: Charles A. Lindbergh* (New York: Harper & Row, 1964), p. 103.
p. 59   Contacts with ...   Lindbergh, *Autobiography of Values*, p. 75.
p. 61   I was furious ...   Ibid, p. 75.
p. 65   "Wu-ll, if ..."   Joyce Milton, *Loss of Eden: A Biography of Charles and Anne Morrow Lindbergh* (New York: HarperCollins, 1993), p. 115.

Chapter Five

p. 67   New York ...   Lindbergh, *The Spirit of St. Louis*.

Chapter Six

p. 85   You are in ...   Milton, *Loss of Eden*, p. 123.
p. 85   I don't know ...   Ibid, p. 123.
p. 89   Even the eight ...   Lindbergh, *Autobiography of Values*, p. 79.
p. 94   ... 132 years ...   Brendan Gill, *Lindbergh Alone*, (New York: Harcourt Brace Jovanovich, 1977), p. 157.
p. 95   I was offered ...   Lindbergh, *Autobiography of Values*, p. 14.
p. 96   I was able ...   Kenneth S. Davis, *The Hero: Charles A. Lindbergh and the American Dream* (Garden City, NY: Doubleday & Company, Inc., 1959), p. 218.

Chapter Seven

p. 99   I was just ...   Milton, *Loss of Eden*, p. 132.
p. 100   "I hope ..."   Ross, *The Last Hero*, p. 151.
p. 101   We must ...   Ibid, p. 151.
p. 102   "The year ..."   Stoff, *Charles A. Lindbergh*, p. vi.
p. 104   I had always ...   Lindbergh, *Autobiography of Values*, p. 117.
p. 105   I saw ...   Anne Morrow Lindbergh, *Bring Me a Unicorn: Diaries and Letters 1922–1928* (San Diego: Harcourt Brace Jovanovich, 1971), p. 89.

p. 106 The second . . . Lindbergh, *Autobiography of Values*, p. 123.

p. 107 My visit . . . Ibid, p. 123.

p. 108 Apparently I am . . . Anne Morrow Lindbergh, *Bring Me a Unicorn*, p. 248.

p. 109 I felt . . . Lindbergh, *Autobiography of Values*, p. 126.

p. 110 To be deeply . . . Anne Morrow Lindbergh, *Hour of Gold, Hour of Lead: Diaries and Letters 1929–1932* (San Diego: Harcourt Brace Jovanovich, 1973), p. 3.

p. 113 When I . . . Ibid, p. 138.

p. 113 And I have . . . Ibid, p. 140.

p. 114 Will you . . . Ibid, p. 163.

p. 114 What you . . . Ibid, p. 186.

p. 117 The baby is . . . Ibid, p. 160.

p. 117 It is good . . . Ibid, p. 204.

p. 118 C. Jr. . . . Ibid, p. 225.

p. 118 The first . . . Ibid, p. 205.

PART TWO

p. 121 Fame . . . Ludovic Kennedy, *The Airman and the Carpenter: The Lindbergh Kidnapping and the Framing of Richard Hauptmann*, (New York: Viking, 1985), p. 40.

Chapter Eight

p. 124 At 7:30 . . . Anne Morrow Lindbergh, *Hour of Gold, Hour of Lead*, p. 226.

p. 125 I had been . . . Lindbergh, *Autobiography of Values*, p. 139.

p. 127 Dear Sir! . . . Milton, *Loss of Eden*, p. 216.

p. 132 This house . . . Anne Morrow Lindbergh, *Hour of Gold, Hour of Lead*, p. 229.

p. 135 Mrs. Anne Morrow . . . George Waller, *Kidnap: The Story of the Lindbergh Case*, (New York: The Dial Press, 1961), p. 24.

p. 135 Mrs. Lindbergh . . . Ibid, p. 24.

p. 137 I offer . . . Jim Fisher, *The Lindbergh Case* (New Brunswick, NJ: Rutgers University Press, 1987), p. 40.

p. 140 Dear Sir . . . Ibid, p. 79.

p. 141 The boy is . . . Ibid, p. 83.

p. 141 "That is . . ." Milton, *Loss of Eden*, p. 251.

p. 142 Friday, May 13 . . . Dorothy Herrmann, *Anne Morrow Lindbergh: A Gift for Life* (New York: Ticknor & Fields, 1992), p. 110.

p. 145 " . . . Life is . . ." Milton, *Loss of Eden*, p. 260.

p. 161 The defense . . . Hermann, *Anne Morrow Lindbergh*, p. 150.

p. 162 "I heard . . ." Waller, *Kidnap*, p. 290.

Chapter Nine

p. 177 I decided . . . Lindbergh, *Autobiography of Values*, p. 144.

p. 179 Your action . . . Davis, *The Hero*, p. 333.

p. 181 We flew . . . Lindbergh, *Autobiography of Values*, p. 113.

p. 181 For me, . . . Anne Morrow Lindbergh, *Locked Rooms and Open Doors: Diaries and Letters 1933–1935* (New York: Harcourt Brace Jovanovich, 1974), p. xvii.

p. 182 Mrs. Lindbergh . . . Mosley, *Lindbergh: A Biography*, p. 168.

p. 183 A final incident . . . Anne Morrow Lindbergh, *Locked Rooms and Open Doors*, p. xxv.

p. 183 The dangers . . . Lindbergh, *The Autobiography of Values*, p. 144.

p. 184 My wife . . . Ibid, p. 145.

p. 185 [It is] unbelievable . . . Davis, *The Hero*, p. 359.

p. 185 The excesses of . . . Ibid, p. 359.

p. 188 There is no . . . Ibid, p. 347.

Chapter Ten

p. 189 . . . Hitler . . . Anne Morrow Lindbergh, *The Flower and the Nettle: Diaries and Letters 1936–1939* (San Diego: Harcourt Brace Jovanovich, 1976), p. 100.

p. 189 No system . . . Davis, *The Hero*, p. 402.

p. 190 The Olympic games . . . Herrmann, *Anne Morrow Lindbergh*, p. 189.

p. 192 I was deeply . . . Lindbergh, *Autobiography of Values*, p. 20, 147.

p. 193 The organized . . . Ibid, p. 147.

p. 193 First impressions . . . Anne Morrow Lindbergh, *The Flower and the Nettle*, p. 83.

p. 193 . . . There is no . . . Ibid, p. 100.

p. 194 Flags hide . . . Ibid, p. 96.

p. 195 Göring was . . . Lindbergh, *Autobiography of Values*, p. 181.

p. 198 I believe . . . Davis, *The Hero*, p. 379.

p. 199 I am . . . Hermann, *Anne Morrow Lindbergh*, p. 199.

p. 200 . . . is some . . . Anne Morrow Lindbergh, *The Wave of the Future: A Confession of Faith* (New York: Harcourt Brace Jovanovich, 1940), p. 15, 37.

Chapter Eleven

p. 203 Knowing the . . . Lindbergh, *Autobiography of Values*, p. 190.

p. 203 . . . I decided . . . Ibid, p. 187.

p. 204 . . . I knew . . . Ibid, p. 192.

p. 205 "If I . . ."   Richard M. Ketchum, *The Borrowed Years 1938–1941: America on the Way to War* (New York: Random House, 1989), p. 639.

p. 206 Various prowar . . .   Lindbergh, *Autobiography of Values*, p. 193.

p. 207 He is . . .   Herrmann, *Anne Morrow Lindbergh*, p. 238.

p. 207 A fleet of . . .   Kenneth S. Davis, *FDR Into the Storm: 1937–1940: A History* (New York: Random House, 1993), p. 553.

p. 209 We shall . . .   Davis, *FDR*, p. 554.

p. 210 Suppose my . . .   Ketchum, *The Borrowed Years*, p. 573.

p. 212 France has . . .   Davis, *The Hero*, p. 400.

p. 213 Few Americans . . .   Wayne S. Cole, *Charles A. Lindbergh and the Battle Against American Intervention in World War II* (New York: Harcourt Brace Jovanovich, 1974), p. 142.

p. 213 The three . . .   Ibid, p. 161.

p. 215 The pressure . . .   Charles A. Lindbergh, *The Wartime Journals of Charles A. Lindbergh* (New York: Harcourt Brace Jovanovich, 1970), p. 481.

p. 215 But no . . .   Milton, *Loss of Eden*, p. 400.

p. 219 I watched . . .   Lindbergh, *Autobiography of Values*, p. 212.

p. 221 In promoting . . .   O'Neill, *A Democracy at War*, p. 49.

Chapter Twelve

p. 223 After my death . . .   Lindbergh, *Autobiography of Values*, p. 402.

p. 225 You know . . .   Milton, *Loss of Eden*, p. 455.

p. 228 We do not . . .   Mosley, *Lindbergh: A Biography*, p. 378.

p. 228 Where civilization . . .   Milton, *Loss of Eden*, p. 445.

BIBLIOGRAPHY

Books:

Ahlgren, Gregory and Stephen Monier, *Crime of the Century: The Lindbergh Kidnapping Hoax*. Boston: Branden Books, 1993.

Allen, Frederick Lewis. *Only Yesterday: An Informal History of the Nineteen Twenties*. New York: Harper & Row, 1964.

————. *Since Yesterday: The 1930s in America*. New York: Harper & Row, 1972.

Beamish, Richard J. *The Story of Lindbergh: The Lone Eagle*. The International Press, 1927.

Behn, Noel. *Lindbergh: The Crime*. New York: The Atlantic Monthly Press, 1994.

Biddle, Wayne. *Barons of the Sky: From Early Flight to Strategic Warfare*. New York: Henry Holt & Company, 1991.

Cole, Wayne S. *Charles A. Lindbergh and the Battle Against American Intervention in World War II*. New York: Harcourt Brace Jovanovich, 1974.

Davis, Kenneth S. *FDR: Into the Storm 1937–1940: A History*. New York: Random House, 1993.

————. *The Hero: Charles A. Lindbergh and the American Dream*. Garden City, NY: Doubleday & Company, Inc., 1959.

Elliott, Robert G. *Agent of Death: Memoirs of an Executioner*. New York: E.P. Dutton & Company, Inc., 1940.

Fife, George Buchanan. *Lindbergh: The Lone Eagle*. New York: The World Syndicate Publishing Co., 1927.

Fisher, Jim. *The Lindbergh Case.* New Brunswick, NJ: Rutgers University Press, 1987.

Freedman, Russell. *The Wright Brothers: How They Invented the Airplane.* New York: Holiday House, 1991.

Gill, Brendan. *Lindbergh Alone.* New York: Harcourt Brace Jovanovich, 1977.

Haines, Lynn and Dora B. Haines. *The Lindberghs.* New York: The Vanguard Press, 1931.

Herrmann, Dorothy. *Anne Morrow Lindbergh: A Gift for Life.* New York: Ticknor & Fields, 1992.

Howard, Fred. *Wilbur and Orville: A Biography of the Wright Brothers.* New York: Alfred A. Knopf, 1987.

Hunter, T. Willard. *The Spirit of Charles Lindbergh: Another Dimension.* Lanham, MD: Madison Books, 1993.

Irey, Elmer L. *The Tax Dodgers: The Inside Story of the T-Men's War with America's Political and Underworld Hoodlums.* New York: Greenburg, 1948.

Kennedy, Ludovic. *The Airman and the Carpenter: The Lindbergh Kidnapping and the Framing of Richard Hauptmann.* New York: Viking, 1985.

Ketchum, Richard M. *The Borrowed Years 1938–1941: America on the Way to War.* New York: Random House, 1989.

Leighton, Isabel, ed. *The Aspirin Age: 1919–1941.* New York: Simon & Schuster, 1949.

Lindbergh, Anne Morrow. *Bring Me a Unicorn: Diaries and Letters 1922–1928.* San Diego: Harcourt Brace Jovanovich, 1971.

———. *Gift from the Sea.* New York: Pantheon Books, 1955.

———. *Hour of Gold, Hour of Lead: Diaries and Letters 1929–1932.* San Diego: Harcourt Brace Jovanovich, 1973.

———. *Locked Rooms and Open Doors: Diaries and Letters 1933–1935.* New York: Harcourt Brace Jovanovich, 1974.

————. *North to the Orient*. New York: Harcourt Brace Jovanovich, 1935.

————. *The Flower and the Nettle: Diaries and Letters 1936–1939*. San Diego: Harcourt Brace Jovanovich, 1976.

————. *War Within and Without: Diaries and Letters 1939–1944*. New York: Harcourt Brace Jovanovich, 1980.

————. *The Wave of the Future: A Confession of Faith*. New York: Harcourt Brace Jovanovich, 1940.

Lindbergh, Charles A. *Autobiography of Values*. San Diego: Harcourt Brace Jovanovich, 1978.

————. *Of Flight and Life*. New York: Charles Scribner's Sons, 1948.

————. *The Spirit of St. Louis*. New York: Charles Scribner's Sons, 1953.

————. *The Wartime Journals of Charles A. Lindbergh*. New York: Harcourt Brace Jovanovich, 1970.

————. *We*. New York: G.P. Putnam's Sons, 1927.

Milton, Joyce. *Loss of Eden: A Biography of Charles and Anne Morrow Lindbergh*. New York: HarperCollins, 1993.

Mosley, Leonard. *Lindbergh: A Biography*. Garden City, NY: Doubleday & Company, Inc., 1976.

O'Brien, P.J. *The Lindberghs: The Story of a Distinguished Family*. International Press, 1935.

O'Neill, William L. *A Democracy at War: America's Fight at Home and Abroad in World War II*. New York: The Free Press, 1993.

Ross, Walter S. *The Last Hero: Charles A. Lindbergh*. New York: Harper & Row, 1964.

Scaduto, Anthony. *Scapegoat: The Lonesome Death of Bruno Richard Hauptmann*. New York: G.P. Putnam's Sons, 1976.

Schlesinger, Arthur M., Jr. *The Age of Roosevelt: The Crisis of the Old Order 1919–1933.* Boston: Houghton Mifflin Company, 1956.

Stoff, Joshua. *Charles A. Lindbergh: A Photographic Album.* New York: Dover Publications, Inc., 1995.

Waller, George. *Kidnap: The Story of the Lindbergh Case.* New York: The Dial Press, 1961.

Whipple, Sidney B. *The Lindbergh Crime.* New York: Blue Ribbon Books, 1935.

Articles:

"Did the Evidence Fit the Crime? The Trial of Bruno Richard Hauptmann is Reconsidered." Tom Zito. *Life,* vol. 5, no. 3 (March 1982): pp. 40–54.

"The Story of the Century: A Close-Up View of the Lindbergh Kidnapping Case." David Davidson. *American Heritage,* vol. XXVII, no. 2 (February 1976): pp. 22–29, 93.

INDEX

Italic page numbers refers to illustrations.

ACKNOWLEDGMENTS

Grateful acknowledgment is made to the following for granting permission to reprint copyrighted material:

From *Anne Morrow Lindbergh: A Gift for Life* by Dorothy Hermann. Copyright © 1992 by Dorothy Hermann. Reprinted by permission of Ticknor & Fields/ Houghton Mifflin Company. All Rights Reserved.

Excerpts from *Autobiography of Values* by Charles A. Lindbergh, Copyright © 1978 by Harcourt Brace & Company and Anne Morrow Lindbergh. Reprinted by permission of the publisher.

Excerpts from *Bring Me a Unicorn: Diaries and Letters of Anne Morrow Lindbergh 1922–1928*. Copyright © 1972 by Anne Morrow Lindbergh. Reprinted by permission of Harcourt Brace & Co.

Excerpt from *Charles A. Lindbergh: A Photographic Album* by Joshua Stoff. Copyright © 1995 by Joshua Stoff. Reprinted by permission of Dover Publications, Inc.

From *Charles A. Lindbergh and the Battle Against American Intervention in World War II* by Wayne S. Cole. Copyright © 1974 by Wayne S. Cole. Reprinted by permission of the author.

Excerpts from *Hour of Gold, Hour of Lead: Diaries and Letters of Anne Morrow Lindbergh 1929–1932*. Copyright © 1973 by Anne Morrow Lindbergh. Reprinted by permission of Harcourt Brace & Co.

From *Kidnap: The Story of the Lindbergh Case* by George Waller. Copyright © 1961 by George Waller. Reprinted by permission of Bantam Doubleday Dell Publishing Group, Inc.

Jim Fisher, *The Lindbergh Case*. Copyright © 1987 by Jim Fisher. Reprinted by permission of Rutgers University Press.

From *Loss of Eden: A Biography of Charles and Anne Morrow Lindbergh* by Joyce Milton. Copyright © 1993 by Joyce Milton. Reprinted by permission of HarperCollins Publishers Inc.

Reprinted with the permission of Scribner, a Division of Simon & Schuster from *The Spirit of St. Louis* by Charles A. Lindbergh. Copyright 1953 by Charles Scribner's Sons; copyright renewed © 1981 by Anne Morrow Lindbergh.

PHOTO CREDITS

Grateful acknowledgment is made to the following for permission to reprint photographs that appear in this book:

Pages 4a and 4b, 32, 191, 225: The Lindbergh Picture Collection, Yale University Library

Back jacket and pages 5, 58, 62, 87, 92, 93, 117, 126, 127, 129, 151, 159, 160, 165, 167, 169, 186, 194, 199, 209, 214: Bettmann News Photos

Pages 7, 9, 13, 15, 16, 30: Minnesota Historical Society

Page 21: Wright State University

Pages 22, 51, 52, 115: National Air and Space Museum

Page 25: Missouri Historical Society

Page 36: Glen Apfelbaum Collection

Page 48: Ev Cassagneres Collection

Pages 53, 95, 190: Culver Pictures, Inc.

Front jacket and pages 60, 64, 89, 90, 105, 152, 153, 157, 158: Brown Brothers

Pages 86, 91, 132, 161, 162, 163, 185, 212, 217, 231: AP/Wide World

Page 112: Cradle of Aviation Museum

Pages 128, 150, 155: New Jersey State Police Museum

Page 196: Zeitgeschichtliches Bildarchiv

Page 229: Richard Brown Collection

Page 230: Robert F. Eisen Collection